ROYAL ENCOUNTERS

PAUL RATCLIFFE

AMBERLEY

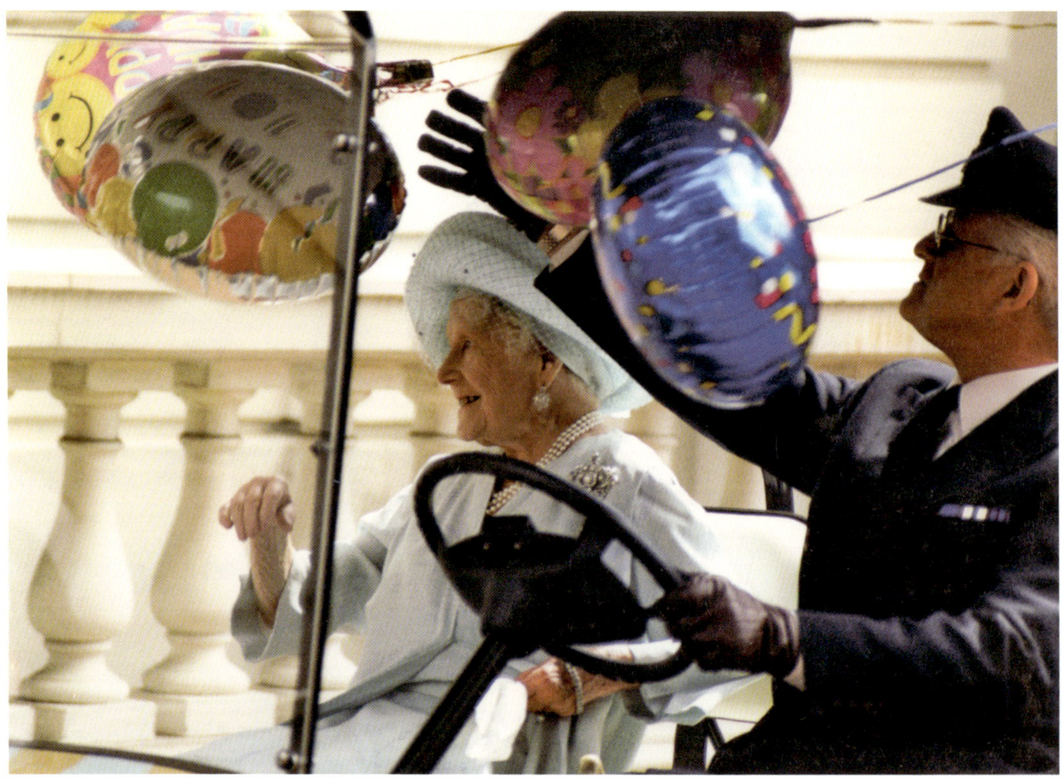

The Queen Mother's 101st birthday.

First published 2011

Amberley Publishing
The Hill, Stroud,
Gloucestershire, GL5 4ER

www.amberley-books.com

British Library Cataloguing in Publication Data.
A catalogue record for this book is available from the British Library.

ISBN 978 1 84868 186 6

Typesetting by Amberley Publishing.
Printed in Great Britain

INTRODUCTION

The British Royal Family holds a special place in the hearts of the public. Worldwide, the day-to-day exploits of the Windsors have kept them at the heart of the nation, and on the covers of numerous books and magazines. From marriages, births, divorces and deaths, every step has been followed with a keen eye and with great interest. It has always been said that a visit by a member of the Royal Family can attract a lot of attention and recognition for charities and good causes, but what about the public? What do they see when a Royal visits their town, city or country?

Royal Encounters, a collection of largely unpublished material, will transform your opinions of the Royals and give you a small insight into their daily lives. The Queen and her extended family every year perform hundreds of engagements and you will see a small glimpse of just what those loyal crowds, all pressed up against the crash barriers, see for themselves. All through the eyes of one photographer, Paul Ratcliffe.

From a young age, Paul Ratcliffe has been going to local appointments to photograph the Royal Family. At the tender age of ten, he was taken with his local school to welcome Charles and Diana, the Prince and Princess of Wales, on their first official visit to the region. And despite the fact that all he could see was a blob in the distance, he was hooked ... Becoming a familiar face in the crowd, and to the Royals themselves, you will love his images. They offer a relaxed and candidly refreshing new approach to Royal publications. With photographs from Royal weddings included, such as the 2005 wedding of TRH the Prince of Wales and the Duchess of Cornwall, surrounded by their family on the steps of St George's Chapel, Windsor, to state events like Trooping the Colour and the Garter Ceremony. Also, local visits by the Queen, princes, dukes and duchesses are all recorded for posterity.

You will also see the fun side of the Royals, from the Duchess of York having a go on a supermarket checkout to just simply showing the Queen as many will have rarely seen her – with a broad, infectious smile that isn't often captured by the camera. Both private and public moments are contained in *Royal Encounters*.

Having been fortunate to meet most of the Royal Family, Paul has also had some revealing conversations over the barriers, particularly with the late Diana, Princess of Wales, who was always on hand to say a cheery, 'Hello Paul ...'. On one occasion, rather poignant now, when she accepted some of his photographs, she replied 'Oh, I never get to keep them. I give them to my boys, so they can remember who their mother is. They put them up next to their beds ...'

Paul's work has been seen in the media worldwide, and he has received two photographic awards in the mid-1990s, his work being highly commended. His first book was published in 1993, and his images have been used on commemorative items and postcards. He has also donated photographs to charities to raise funds for good causes. Indeed, when the Royal Household cricket team needed an image of the Queen to grace the cover of their charity publication, one of Paul's photographs was used, and the Queen herself sanctioned her approval when selecting it. Praise indeed!

Paul Ratcliffe

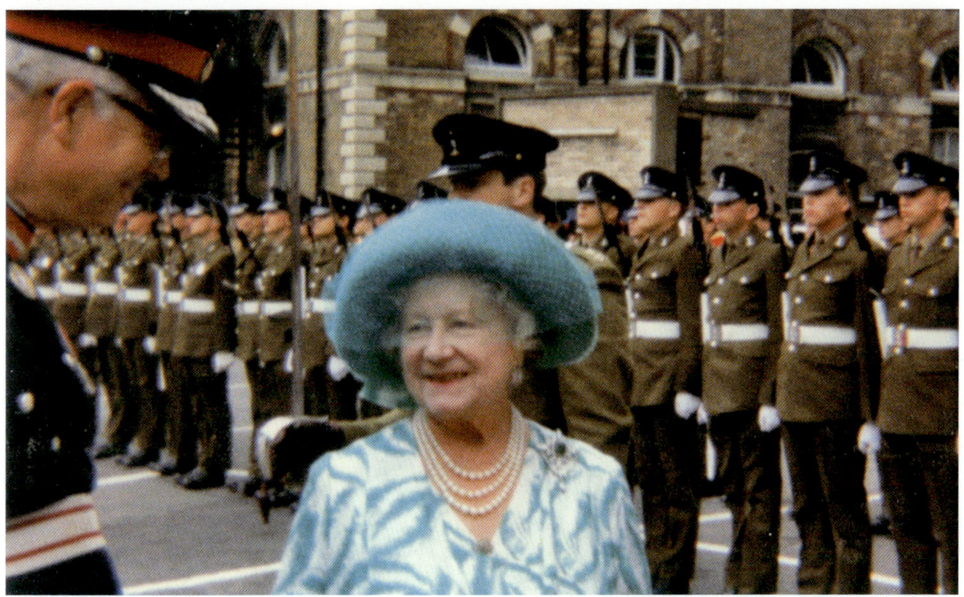

The Queen Mother, York, 24 June 1987
For her visit to York, the Queen Mother arrived at the city's railway station to a Guard of Honour in the Tea Room Square forecourt. She then travelled to the nearby Minster to officially unveil a memorial to the Battle of Kohima, and to take a march-past from veterans from the campaign in the Far East.

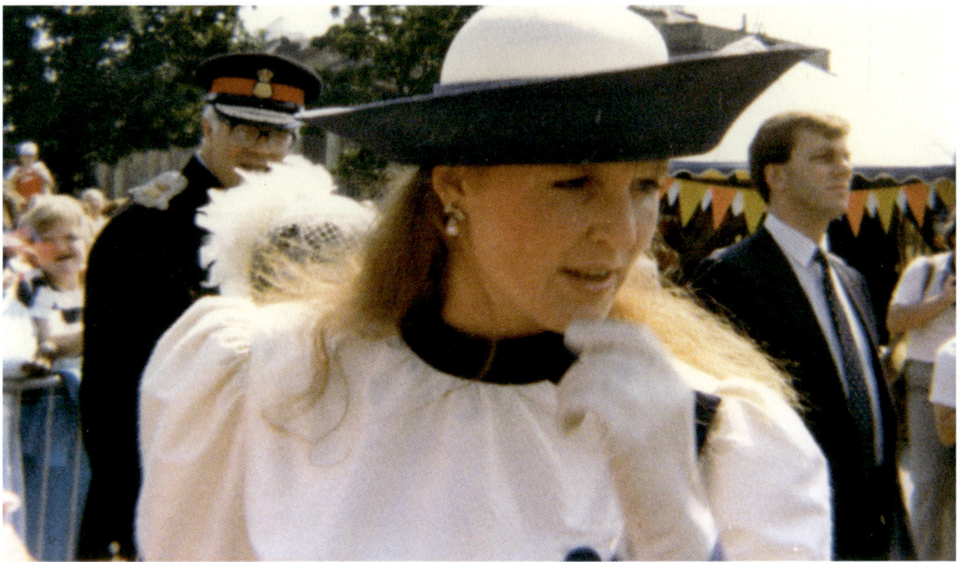

The Duchess of York, York, 4 July 1987
Along with her husband, this was the first official visit the Duchess made to the city that bears her title, visiting the Minster and Castle Museum. Here she greeted the crowds that thronged on that hot summer day, me included as I was celebrating my sixteenth birthday! At one point she crossed paths with the Duke whilst they were walking around – jokingly they both extended their hands to each other – 'I'm Sarah', and 'I'm Andrew', they laughed.

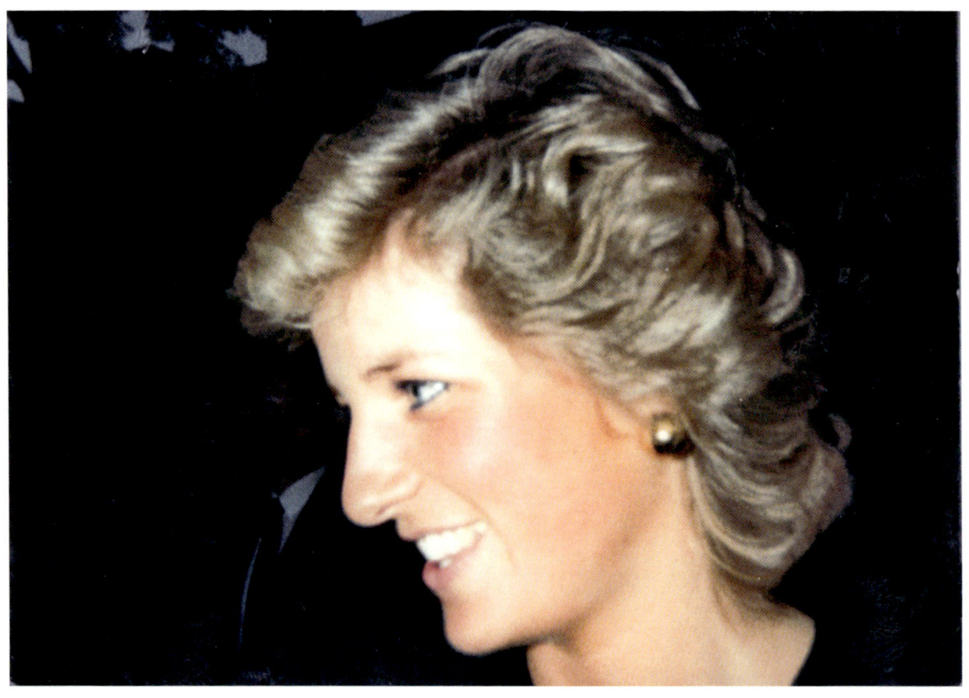

Diana, Princess of Wales, Doncaster, 9 October 1987
The Princess visited Doncaster to see the marriage guidance offices in the city, and looked particularly tanned after a recent holiday.

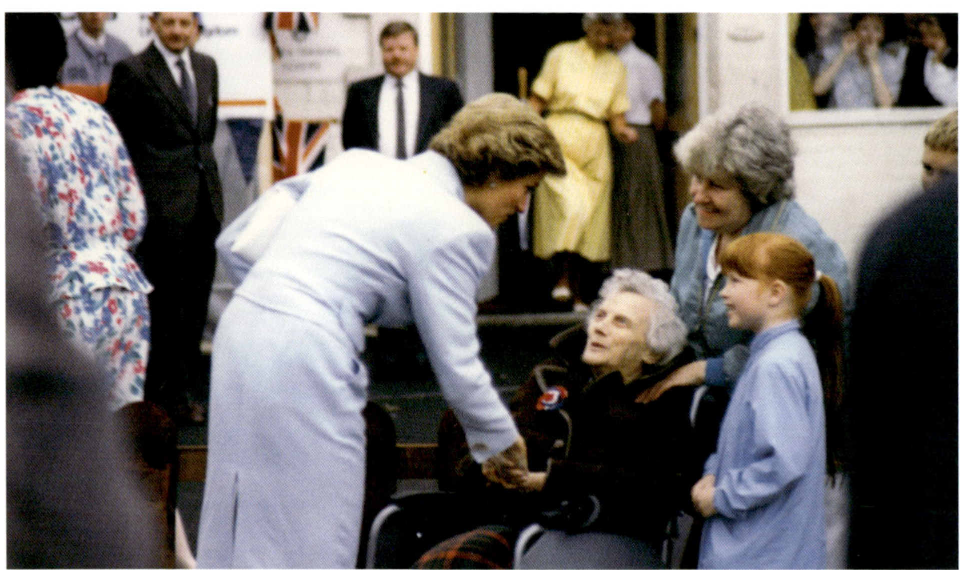

Diana, Princess of Wales, Whitley Bay, 21 July 1988
The northern seaside town of Whitley Bay welcomed the Princess as she visited a Youth Training Scheme at a Barnardo's centre, and she stopped to chat to a elderly lady with her family. It was here that I plucked up the courage to ask if I could kiss her. 'Well, you better kiss my hand, you never know what a kiss on the cheek may lead to', she flirtingly replied.

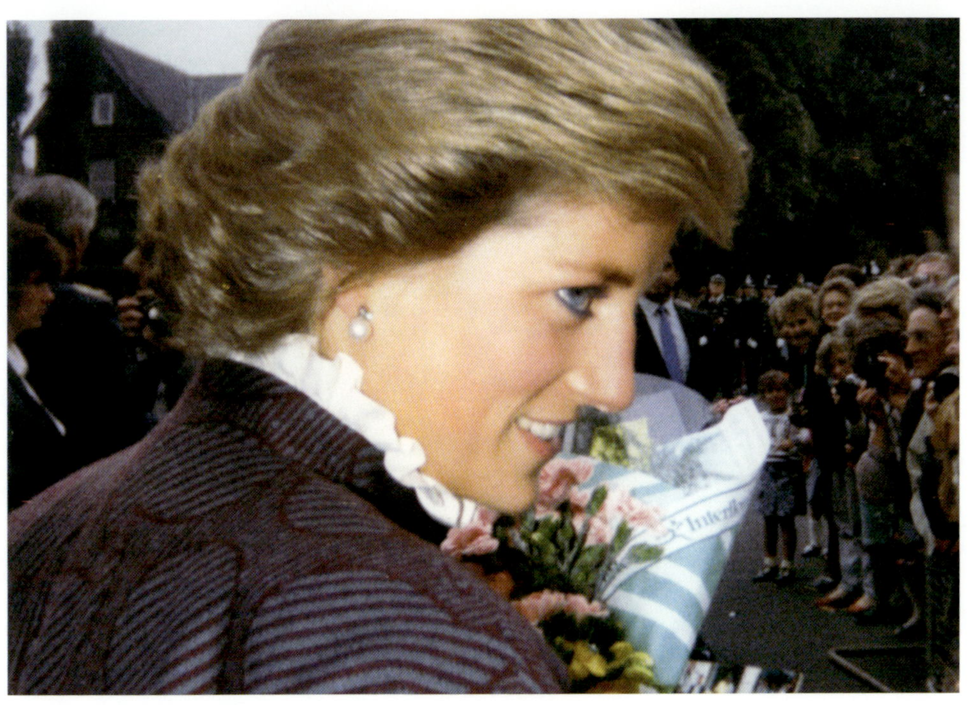

Diana, Princess of Wales, Leeds, 21 September 1988
As president of the children's charity Barnardo's, the Princess stopped off at their Horsforth offices. As usual, large crowds had thronged outside and a lengthy walkabout ensued. I had presented a picture (from her previous visit) to the Princess, much to her obvious delight.

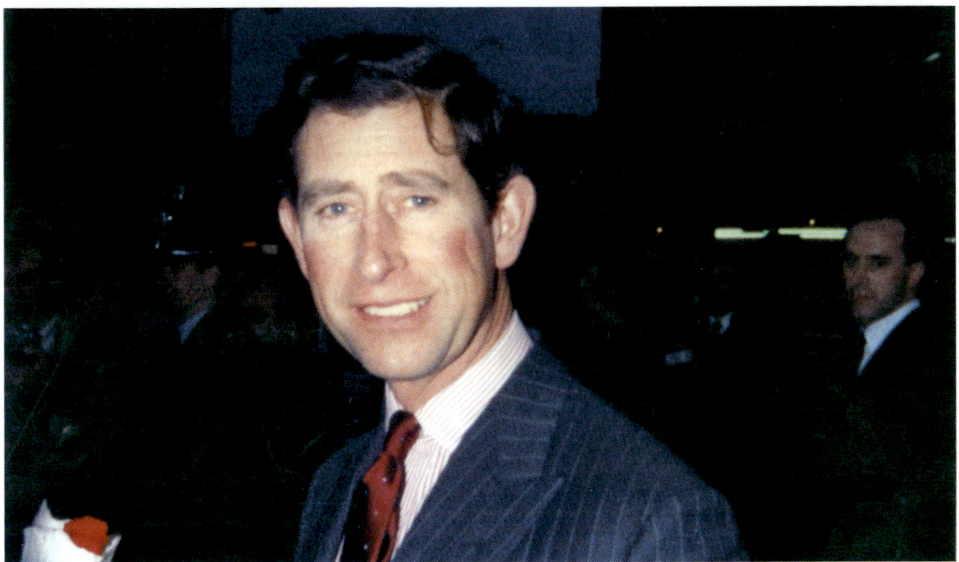

Prince Charles, Bradford, 14 February 1989
It was a St Valentine's Day visit for the Prince to Bradford, to see at first hand their Business Enterprise Centre and the young entrepreneurs. It was late afternoon when he finally met the crowds, and he couldn't resist posing for a photograph as he left!

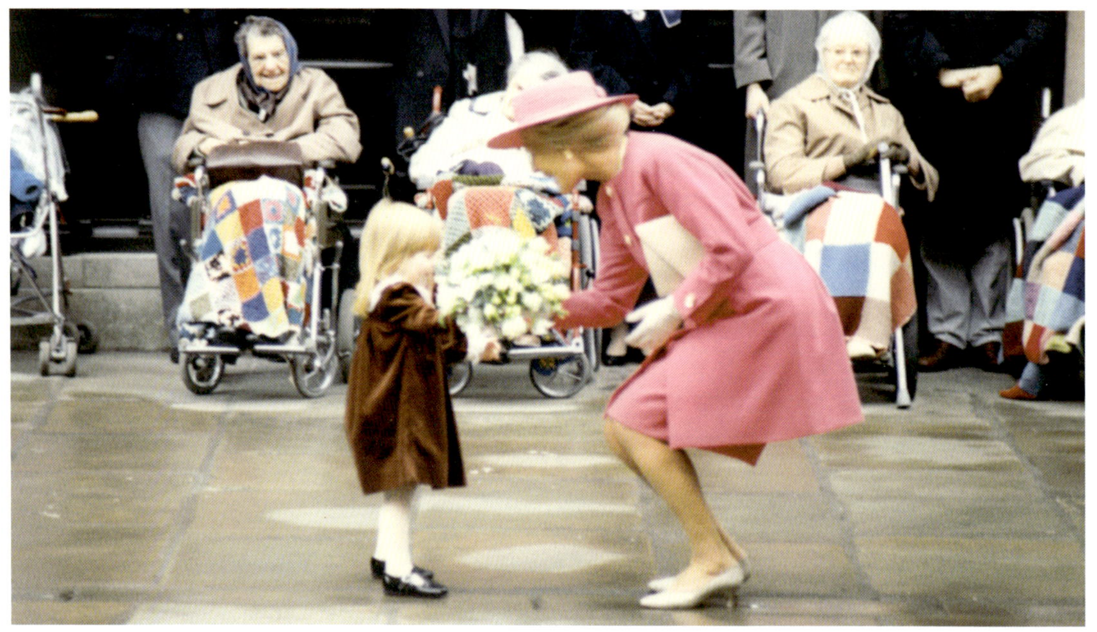

Katharine, Duchess of Kent, York, 22 April 1989

The Yorkshire-born Duchess of Kent visited York to be made a Freeman of the City. Her family has long associations with the region, and her brother, Sir Marcus Worsley, was for a long time one of its Lord Lieutenants – the Queen's official representative in the area. Here she receives a posy from a little girl outside the Mansion House.

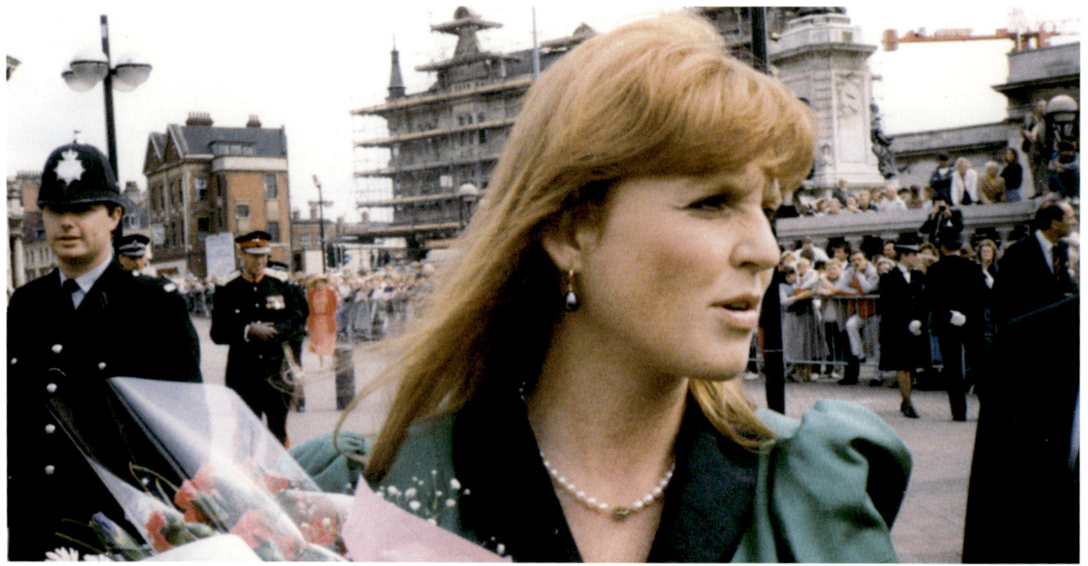

The Duchess of York, Hull, 5 June 1989

Looking fresh in a long green dress, the Duchess visited Hull one summer morning. 'I bet you thought I wasn't going to come over then', the Duchess teased as she criss-crossed the crowds. One of the crowd enquired after her daughter (Princess Beatrice – then nearly one year old), and she said she had 'left her eating toast and honey, and missing her mum!'

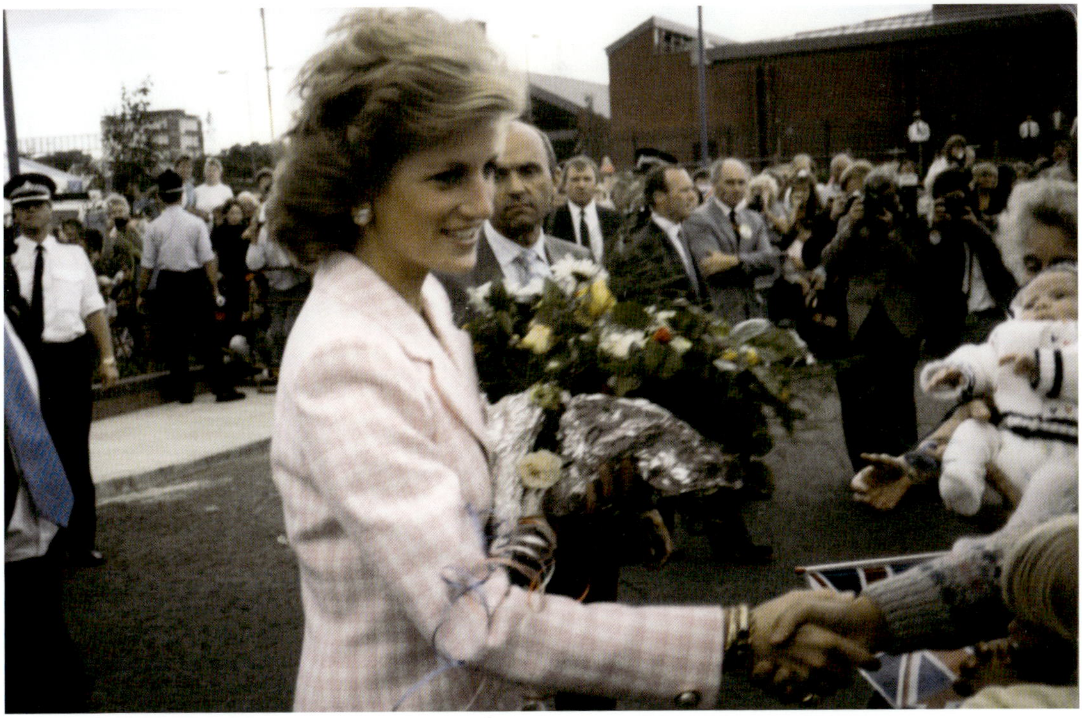

Diana, Princess of Wales, Leeds, 27 July 1989
Visiting the offices of National Breakdown Recovery Club in Pudsey, it was a pink gingham coat dress that wowed her fans as she shook hands – particularly with the many babies she was offered to hold.

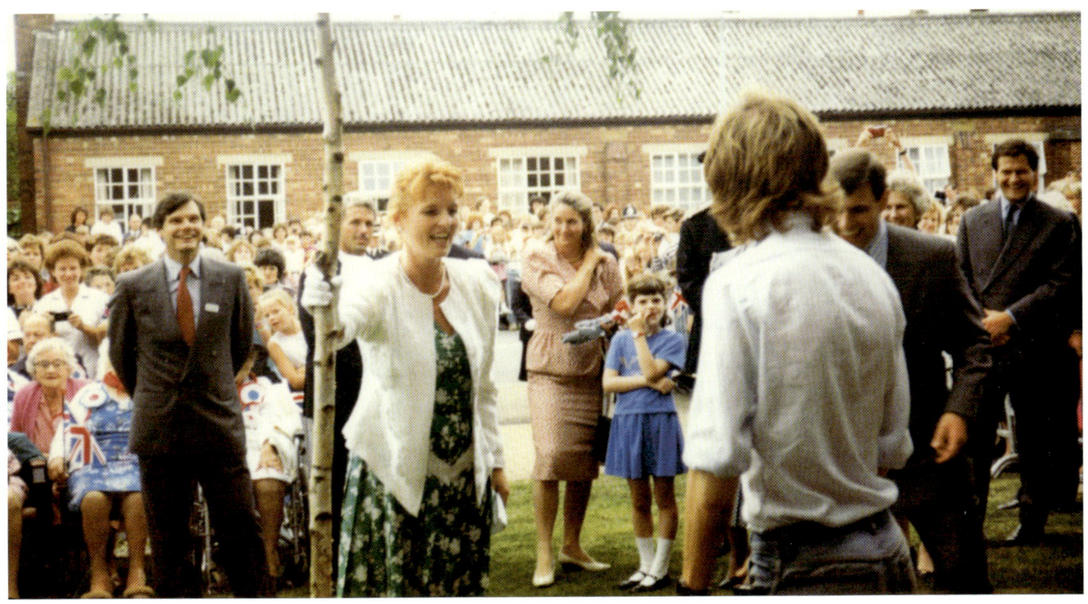

The Duke and Duchess of York, Northallerton, 2 August 1989
The Royal couple planted a tree in the grounds of the Friarage Hospital in Northallerton to mark their visit, with the Duchess offering to turn gardener for the day and assist in holding the tree trunk!

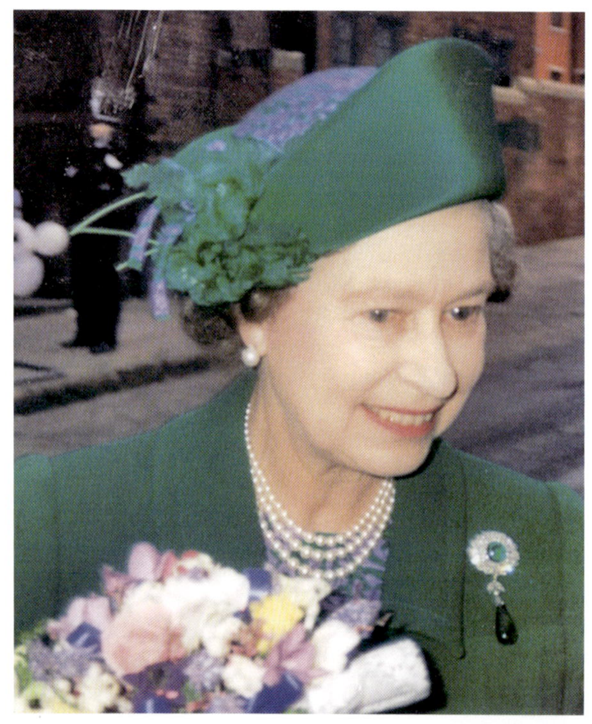

The Queen, Leeds, 23 February 1990
Crowds turned out in force to see the Queen on her first visit to Leeds for many years, and her visit to St Aidan's church in Harehills proved popular for young and old alike as she walked past, accepting flowers and gifts.

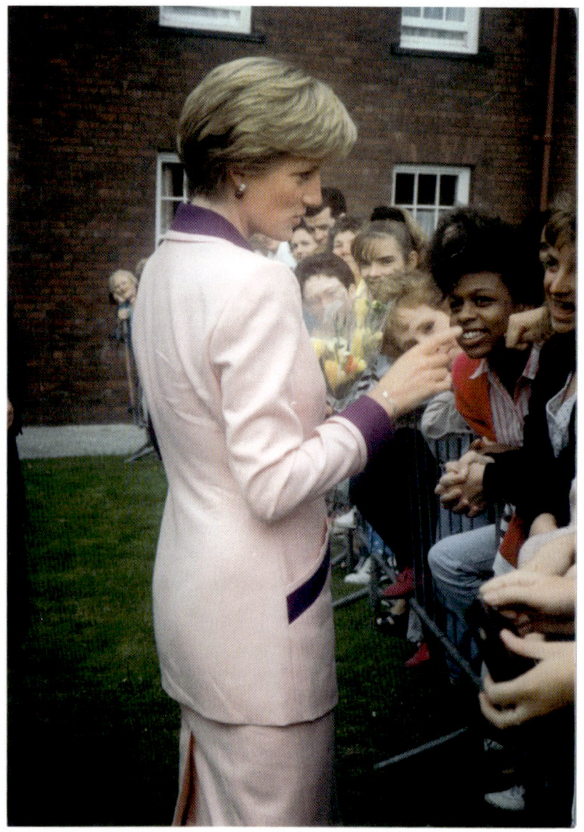

Diana, Princess of Wales, Liverpool, 11 September 1990
The world-famous Liverpool Alder Hey Hospital welcomed Princess Diana as she visited the National Meningitis Trust's research projects.

**The Duchess of York, Derby,
14 February 1991**

Valentine's red for the Duchess on her
February visit! I had got a new camera and
was still trying to learn how to use it – 'How's
the camera working?' she enquired. 'Do you
want to take a picture of me? Try pressing
that.' She added, 'Turn it off and on again;
that always works', offering a cheeky smile.
'Yes! Well done.' Here, she is calling over to
the crowds to say goodbye before she got
back into her car.

**Diana, Princess of Wales, Harrogate,
19 March 1991**

'Surprise, surprise – mustn't say that, makes
me sound like Cilla', the Princess exclaimed
on seeing me. She visited Harrogate to
open the new £6 million offices of Ackrill
Newspapers – before one excited young girl
gave her a painting she had specially done
for her.

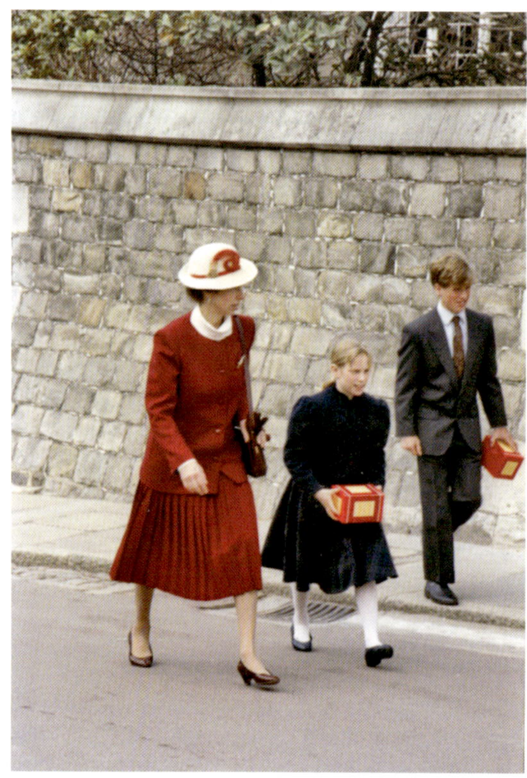

HRH, The Princess Royal and her children, Peter and Zara Phillips, Windsor, 31 March 1991

Traditionally, the Royal Family stays at Windsor during the Easter break, and after the service the Royal Family take sherry with the Dean. Princess Anne and her two young children, Peter and Zara Phillips, walk back to the castle through the Lower Ward Precincts, Easter eggs safely held in their hands.

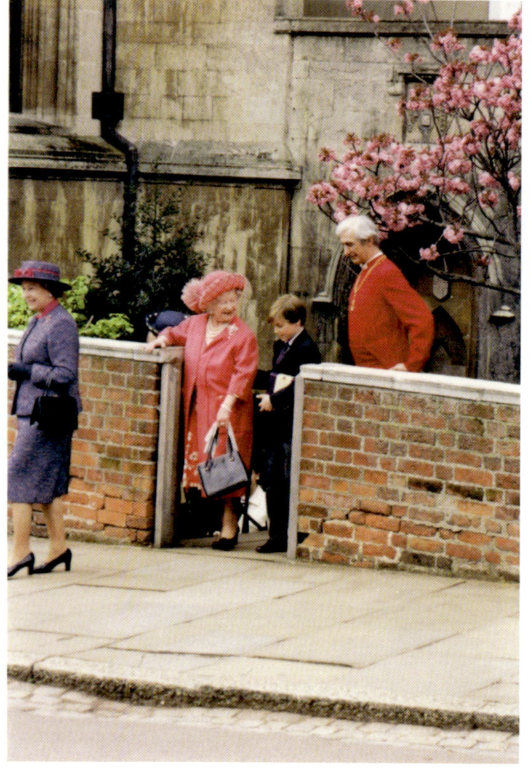

The Queen, The Queen Mother and Prince William, St George's Chapel, Windsor, 19 April 1991

In a scene that was so touching, the young Prince William helped his great-grandmother up the steps of the Deanery. Prince William later commented that images similar to this one were amongst his favourites of him and the Queen Mother.

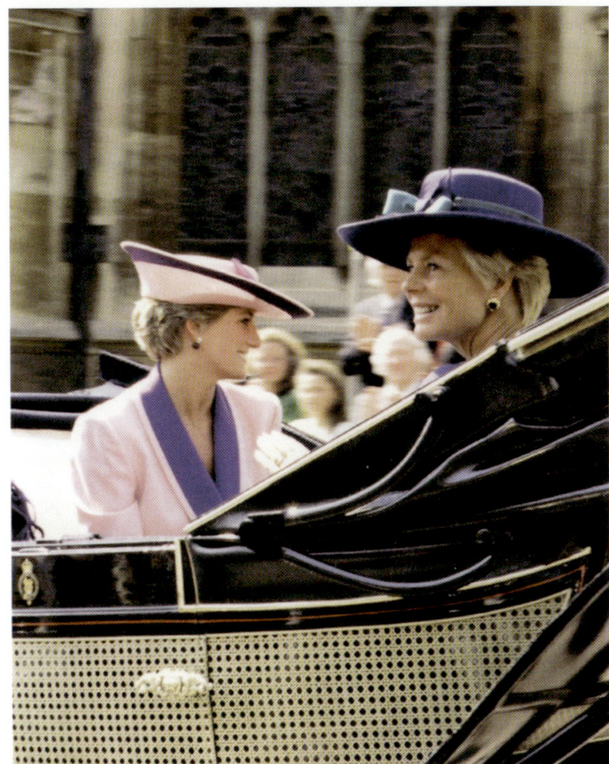

Diana, Princess of Wales, and Katharine, Duchess of Kent, the Garter Ceremony, Windsor Castle, 17 June 1991
The Princess of Wales (as a Garter Wife) rides back to the castle with the Duchess of Kent.

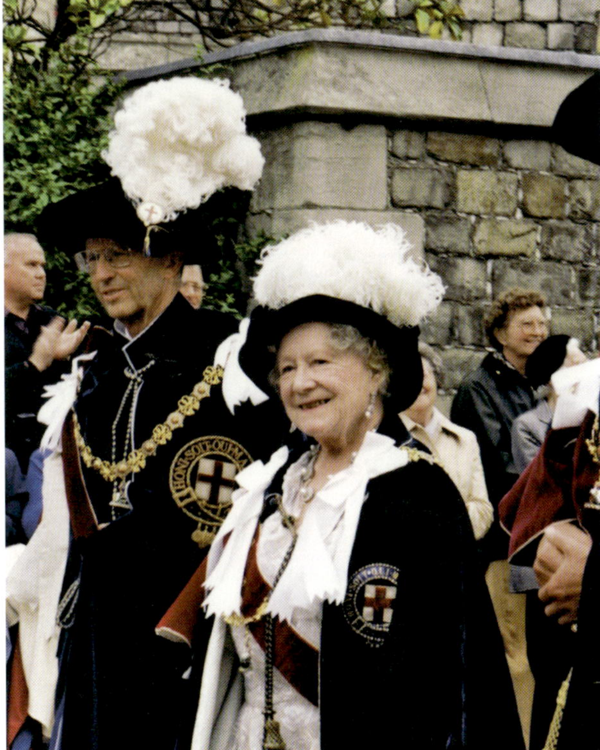

The Queen Mother with the then King of Belgium, King Baudouin, at the Garter Ceremony, Windsor Castle, 1991
The Order dates back to 1348, and every year the Queen and the Royal Knights of the Order process down the Lower Ward of the Precincts of Windsor Castle to the service in St George's Chapel. Here the Queen Mother is pictured with Baudoin, King of the Belgians (who was installed as a Knight that day).

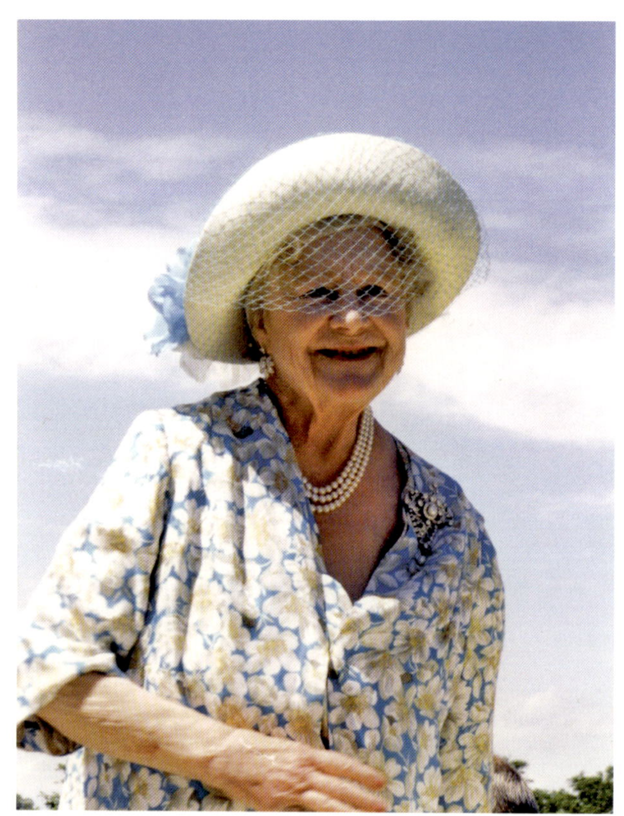

Royal Ascot, 21 June 1991
The Queen Mother and Duchess of
York steal the limelight from the other
Royal ladies at the Royal Meeting in
bright colours, the Duchess showing
off her hat on her Ladies' Day
appearance!

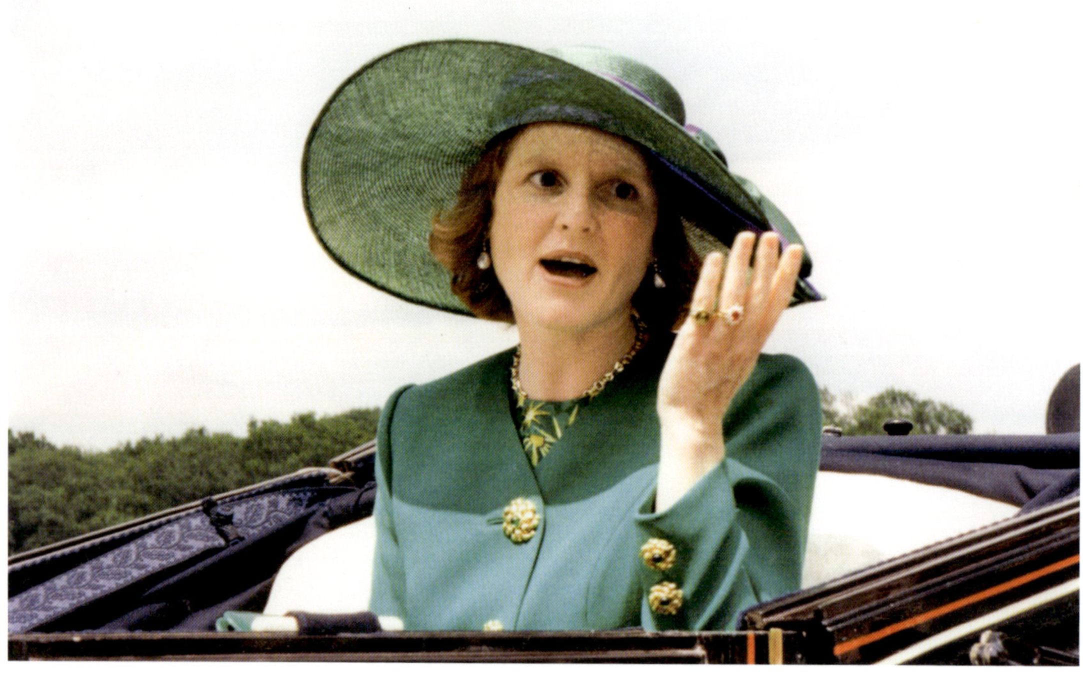

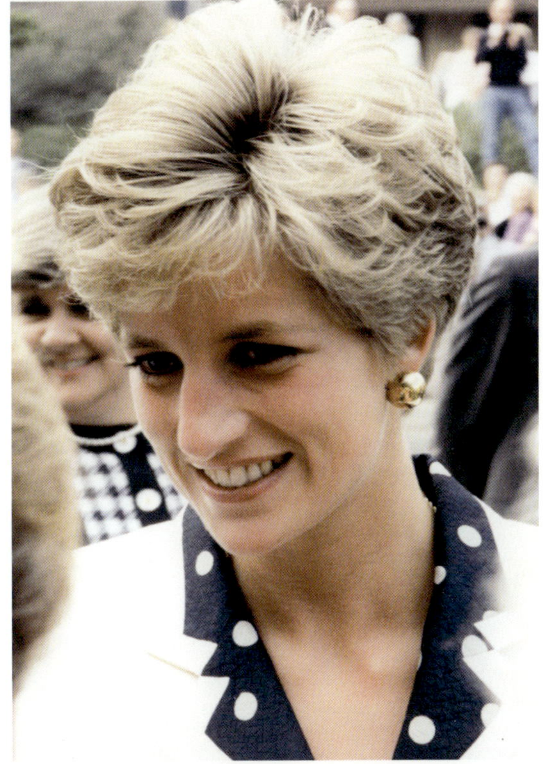

**Diana, Princess of Wales, Shipley,
12 September 1991**

It was a series of engagements for the
Princess, starting at the Shipley Resource
Centre (and the obligatory Royal walkabout),
before ending her day with a visit to St
Gemma's Hospice in nearby Leeds. The visit
was rescheduled from the previous summer
as Prince William had suffered a head injury
while at school.

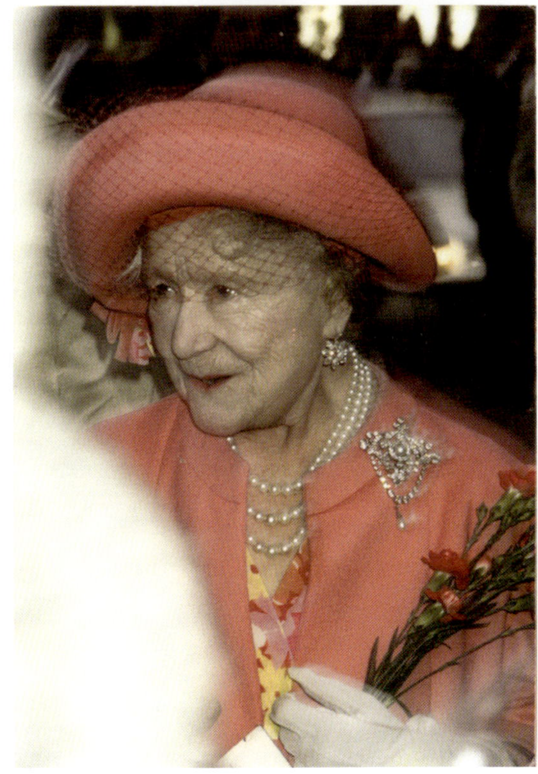

**The Queen Mother, Feren's Art Gallery,
Hull, 31 October 1991**

On a bitterly cold and windy day, the Queen
Mother, in bright pink, brought some colour
to the area as she met crowds after visiting
Hull's Feren's Art Gallery to open the new
extension. It was her first visit to the city
since the Blitz in the Second World War.

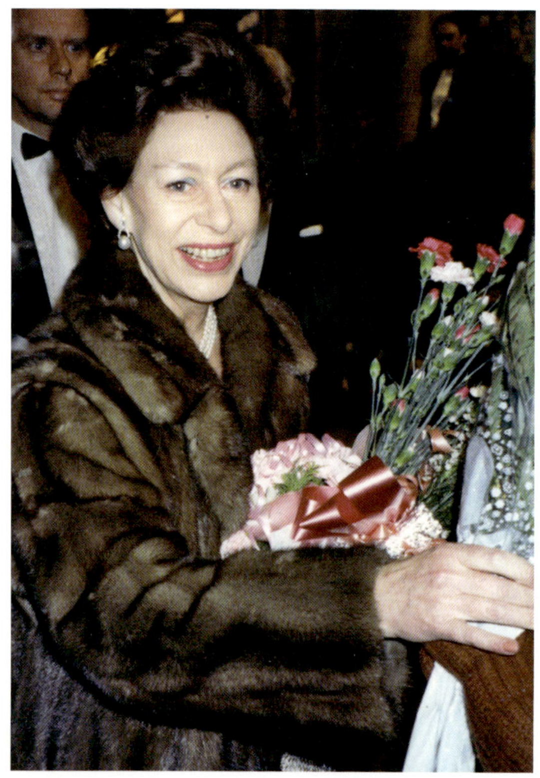

Princess Margaret, Leeds, 8 February 1992
Wrapped up warmly and elegantly in her fur coat, the Princess arrived at the Leeds Grand Theatre to see the Premiere of the Northern Ballet Theatre's *Swan Lake.*

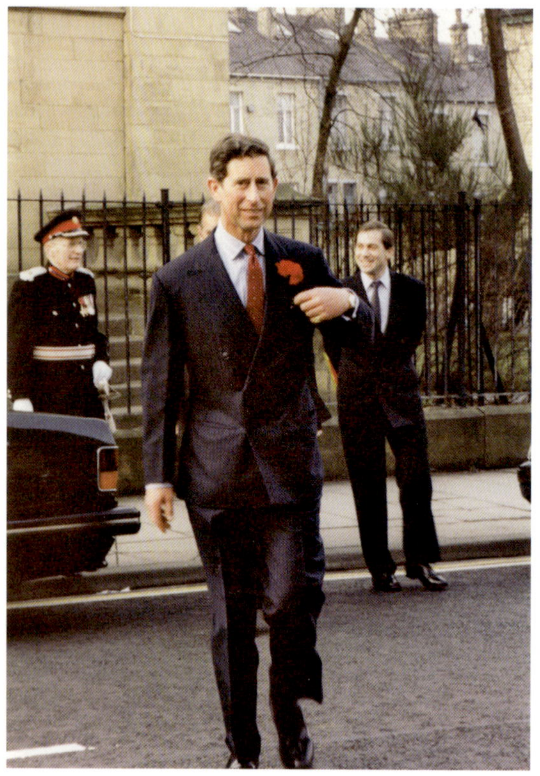

Prince Charles, Bradford, 26 February 1992
The Prince visited the Marlborough Road doctor's surgery in the Manningham area of Bradford as President of the Royal College of General Practioners, before crossing the road to speak to the well-wishers that had waited patiently behind the crowd control barriers.

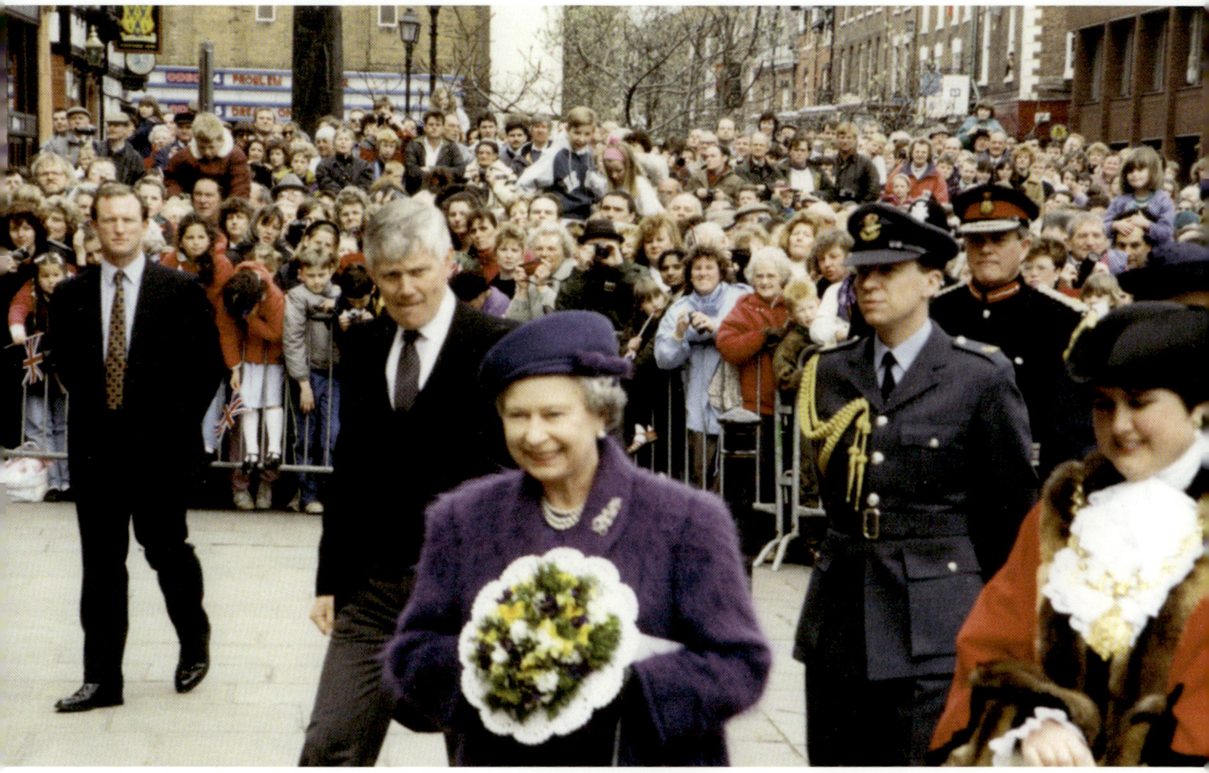

Above:

The Queen, Chester, 16 April 1992
The Royal Maundy attracted the
Queen and Prince Philip, and here,
in Chester's city centre enormous
crowds turned out to see her.

Right:

**Princes Charles, Edward and
Andrew, St George's Chapel,
19 April 1992**
After a quick sherry in the Deanery,
the three Royal Princes, Charles,
Andrew and Edward, all had a quick
joke with the Dean before they left
for lunch at Windsor Castle.

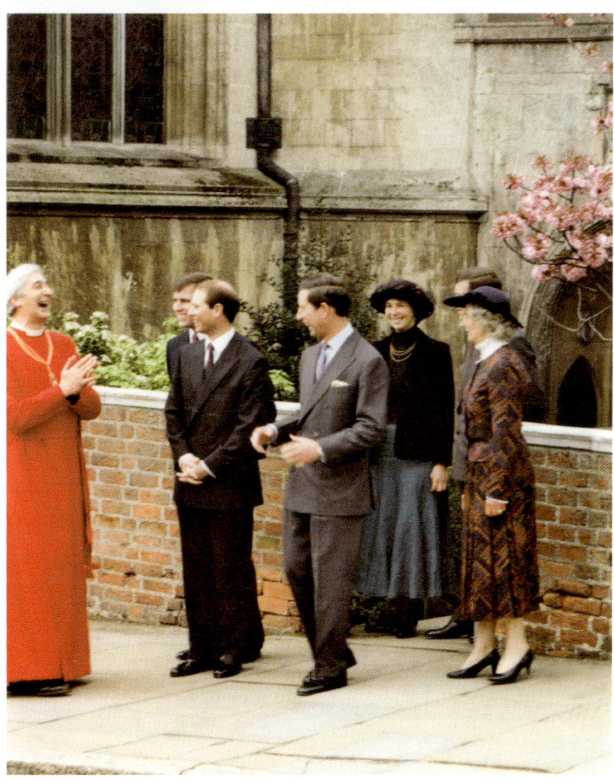

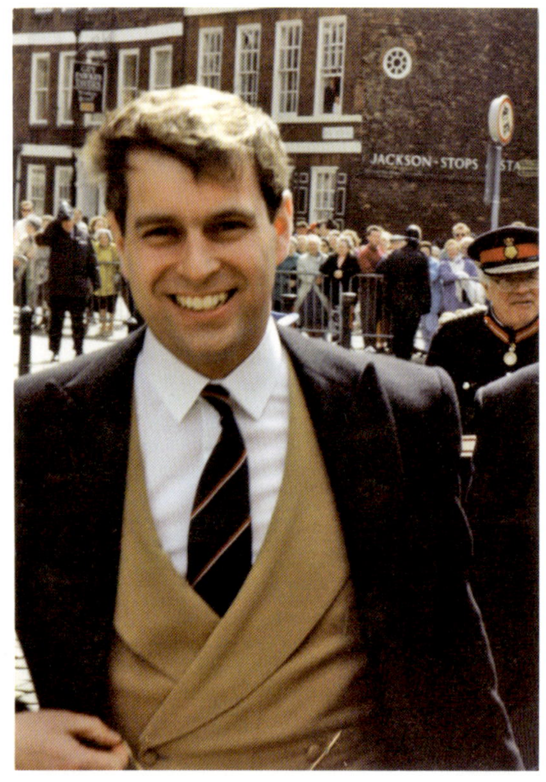

Prince Andrew, York, 1 May 1992
Wearing his morning suit, the Prince breezed past onlookers to attend a service marking the millennium of the Shrievalty at York Minster.

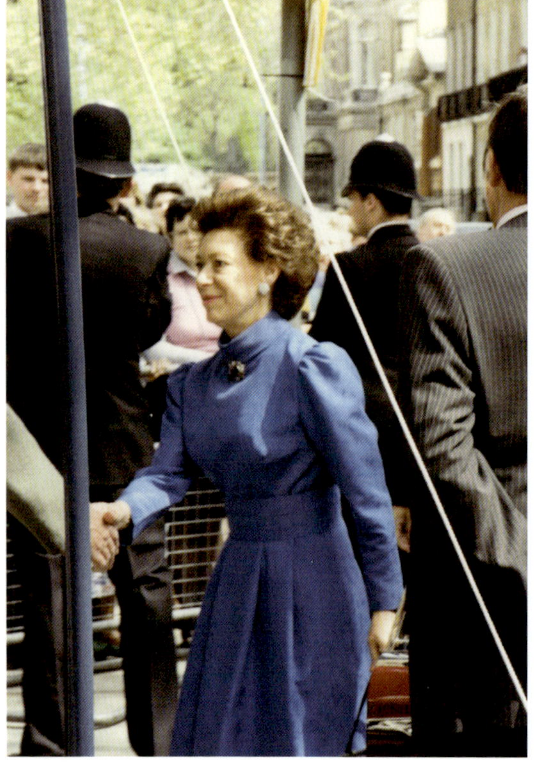

Princess Margaret, London, 7 May 1992
Alongside her mother and sister, Princess Margaret attended the reunion for officers who served on HMS *Vanguard*, at London's Caledonian Club. It was on HMS *Vanguard* that the Royal Family sailed on their famous tour of South Africa some forty-five years previously.

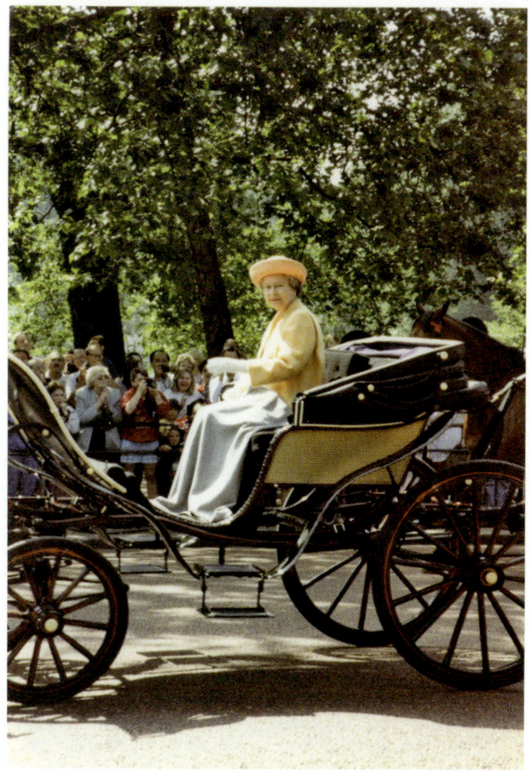

Trooping the Colour London, 13 June 1992
A young Prince Harry smiles from the
carriage carrying his mother and great-
grandmother as they travel back to
Buckingham Palace after watching the Queen's
official birthday parade in Horse Guards
Parade (left). Meanwhile, the Queen waves
at the crowd from her phaeton carriage as
she is driven down The Mall (above). The
Royal Family had been subjected to an intense
amount of press speculation following the
publication of Andrew Morton's book on
Princess Diana. While the Royal couple put
on a brave face in front of the cameras that
day, it must have nevertheless been a personal
strain, particularly for the young Prince.

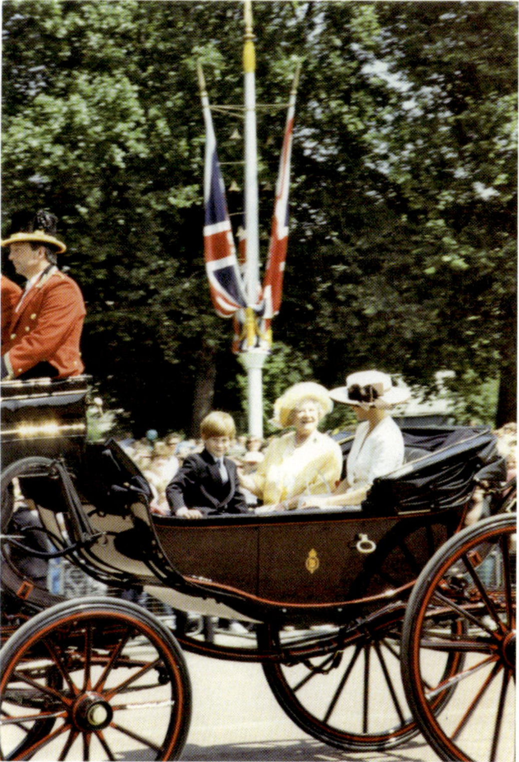

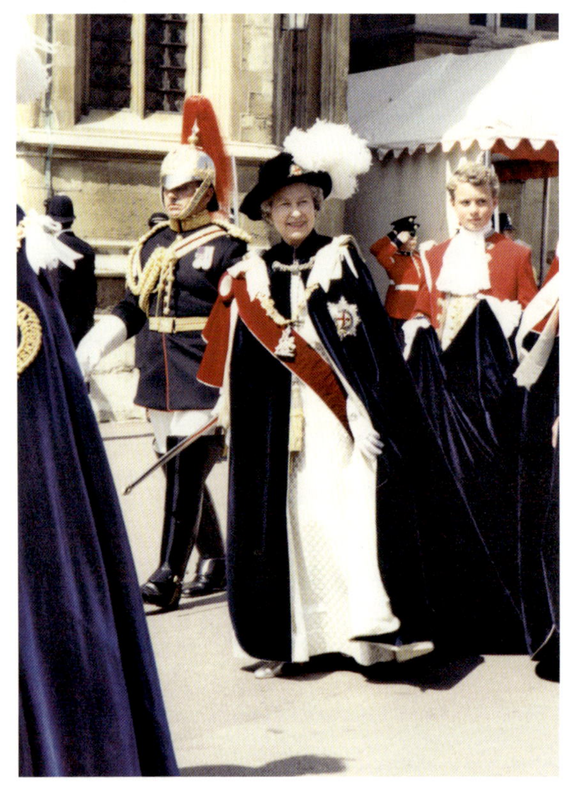

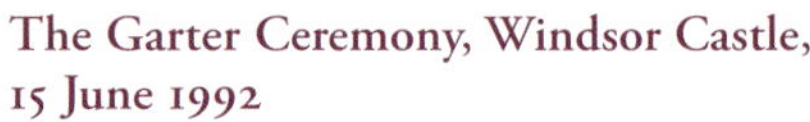

**The Garter Ceremony, Windsor Castle,
15 June 1992**
Both the Queen and Prince Charles look
resplendent in their velvet robes and hats
topped with ostrich plumes as they walk
past the invited crowds for the Order of the
Garter Ceremony.

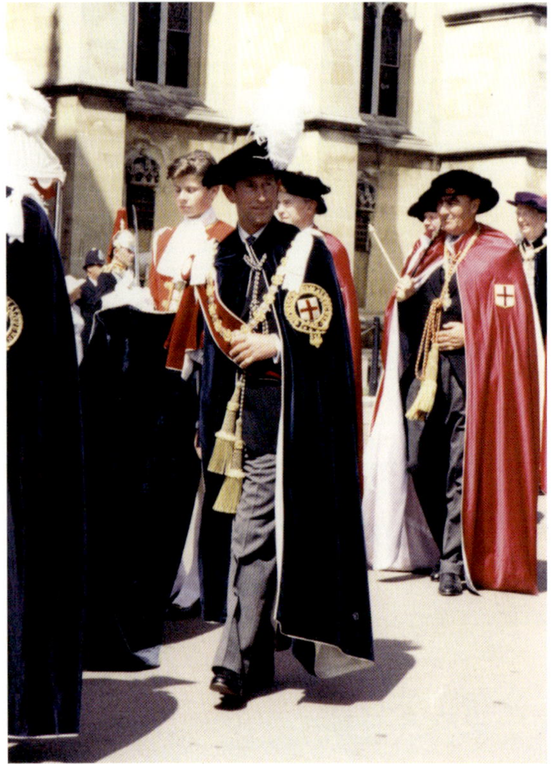

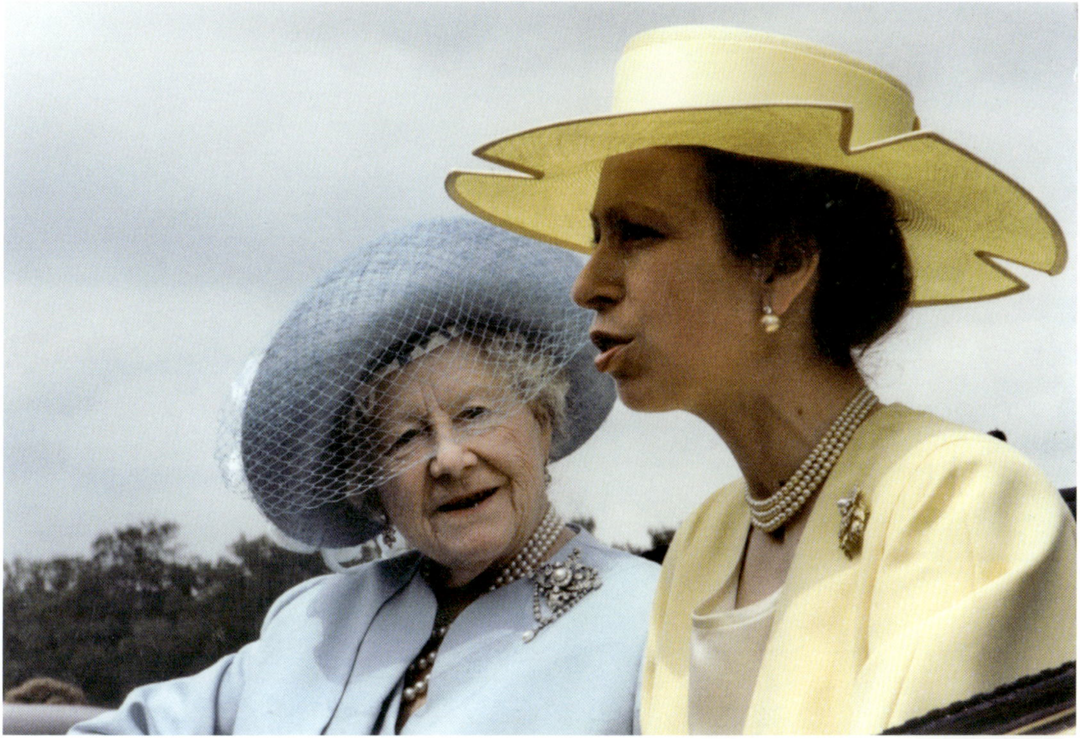

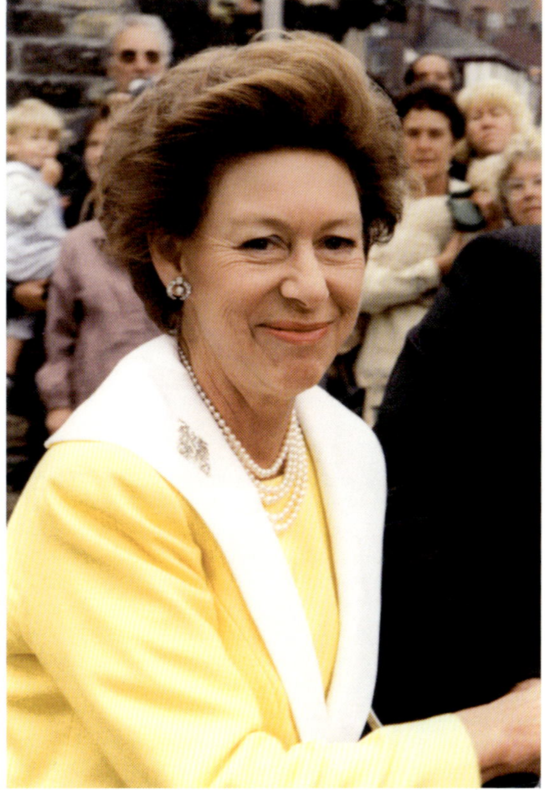

The Queen Mother and Princess Anne, Windsor, 18 June 1992
With her grandmother by her side, Princess Anne sported a yellow flower hat for her Ladies' Day appearance, whilst the Queen Mother opted for pale blue.

Right:
Princess Margaret, Sheffield, 2 July 1992
The Princess visited the Wilson Carlile Church Army College of Evangelism in Sheffield, and looked radiant in yellow.

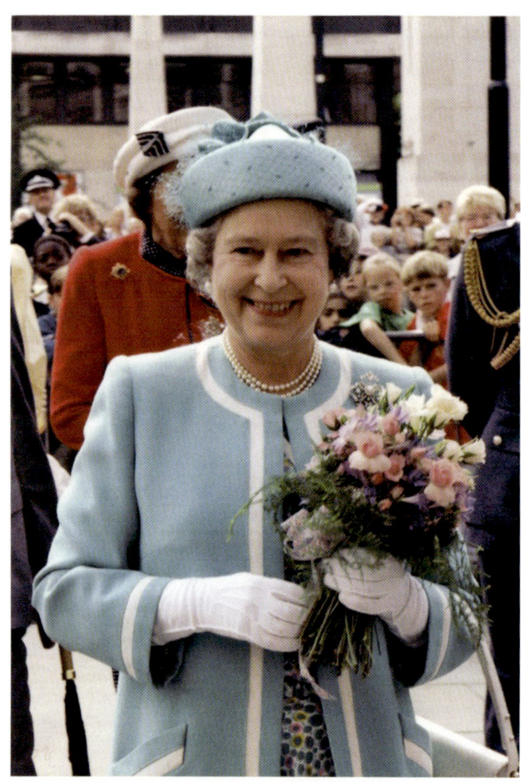

The Queen, Manchester, 17 July 1992
After officially opening Manchester's new Metrolink Tramway system in St Peter's Square, the Queen meets crowds who have thronged the city centre to catch a glimpse of her. She later travelled on a tram to nearby Bury for a lunch at the Town Hall.

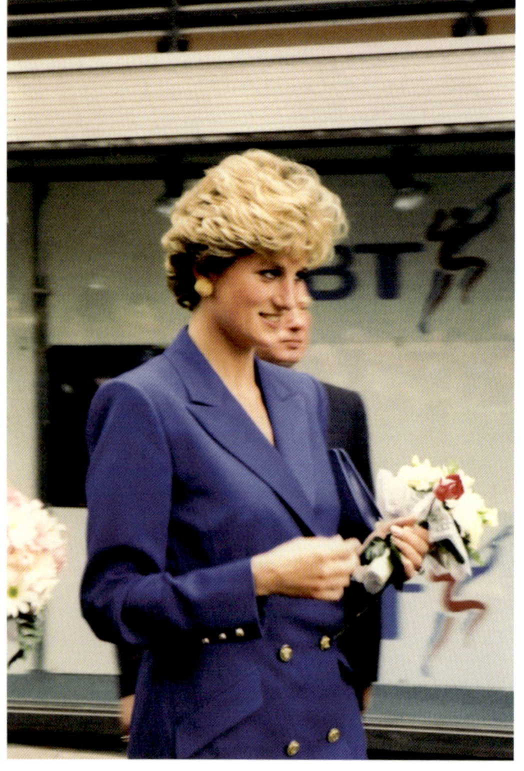

Diana, Princess of Wales, Nottingham, 9 September 1992
The Prince and Princess undertook a variety of engagements in Nottingham. Here, the Princess visited Help the Aged's 'Daybreak' bus in the city centre – 'He's an expert photographer. He's my Photographer Royal', she joked to a lady standing next to me. 'He always takes such fantastic photos', she added.

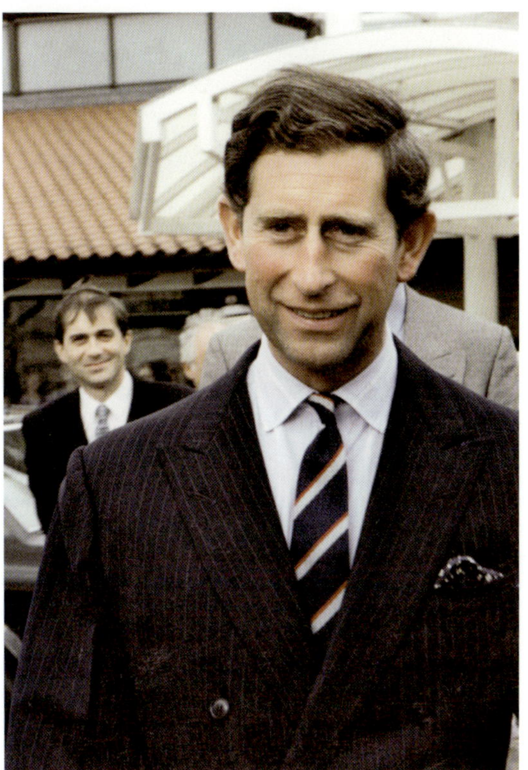

**Prince Charles, Nottingham,
9 September 1992**
Meanwhile, the Prince leaves the University of
Nottingham after opening the £5 million Arts
Centre. 'Is it easy to operate your camera?' he
asked. 'They're quite a funny shape aren't they?'

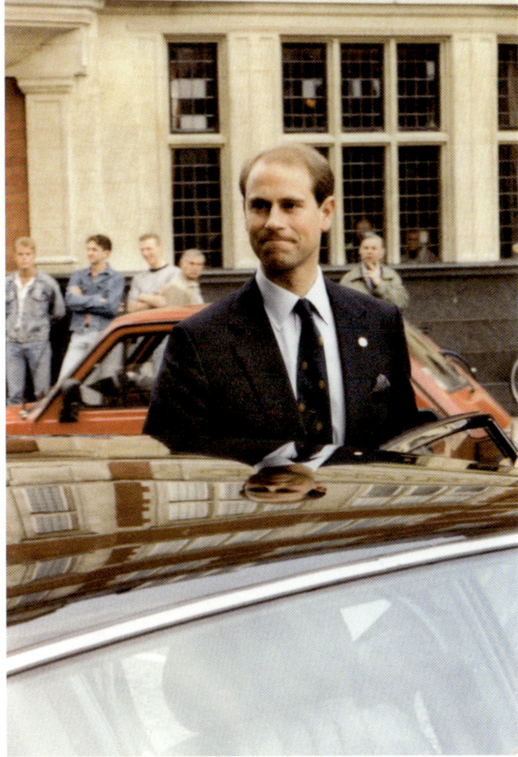

**Prince Edward, The Guildhall, Hull,
26 September 1992**
A series of visits brings the Prince to Hull,
where he visits the Prince's Quay shopping
centre for a visit to the Duke of Edinburgh
'Key Challenge', and he later visited the
Guildhall for a lunch in his honour. When
someone offered their hand to shake, the
Prince wryly joked, 'I can't shake hands, as I'd
then have to shake everyone's hand and it's
starting to wear away!'

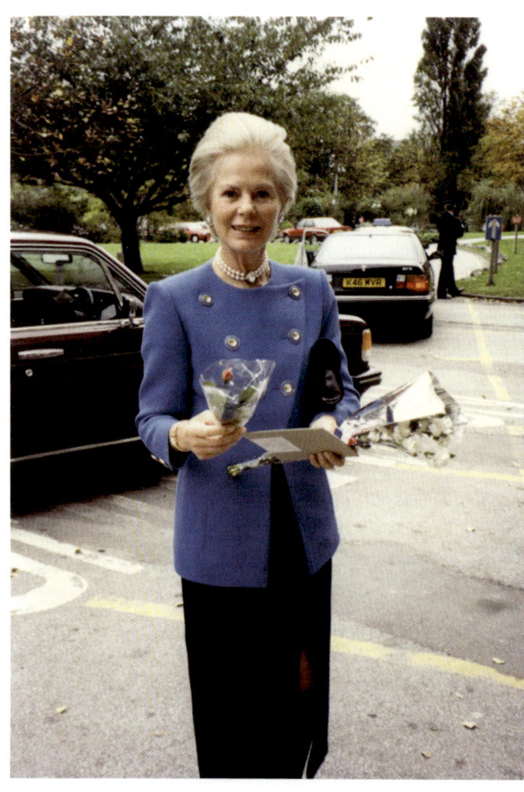

**Katharine, Duchess of Kent, Manchester,
5 October 1992**
The Duchess poses for a photograph outside
the Christie Hospital in Manchester.

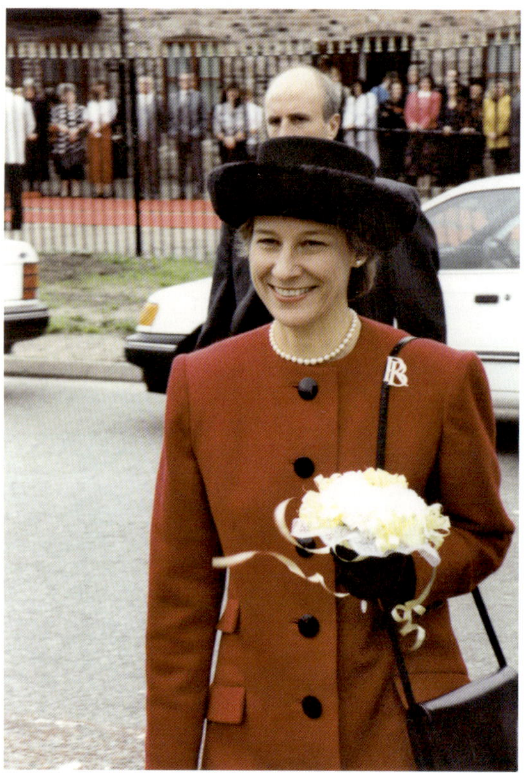

**The Duchess of Gloucester, Kirkby,
6 October 1992**
The popular minor Royal, the Duchess of
Gloucester visited Merseyside to see the Tower
Hill Enterprise Centre in Kirkby. She wore
a brooch with the initials R and B entwined
– the initials of herself and her husband,
Richard and Birgitte.

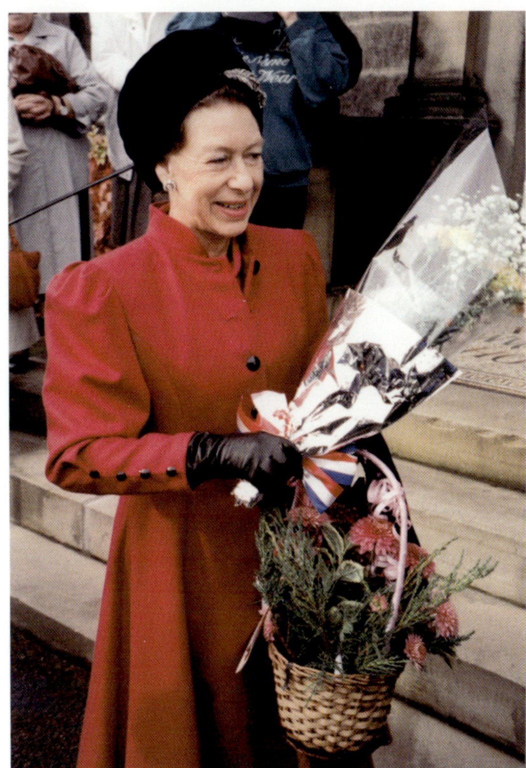

Princess Margaret, Harrogate, 26 October 1992
The Princess visited the Northern Police Convalescent Home in the spa town of Harrogate. 'It looks like a big garden', she joked to her lady-in-waiting on seeing well-wishers with flowers for her.

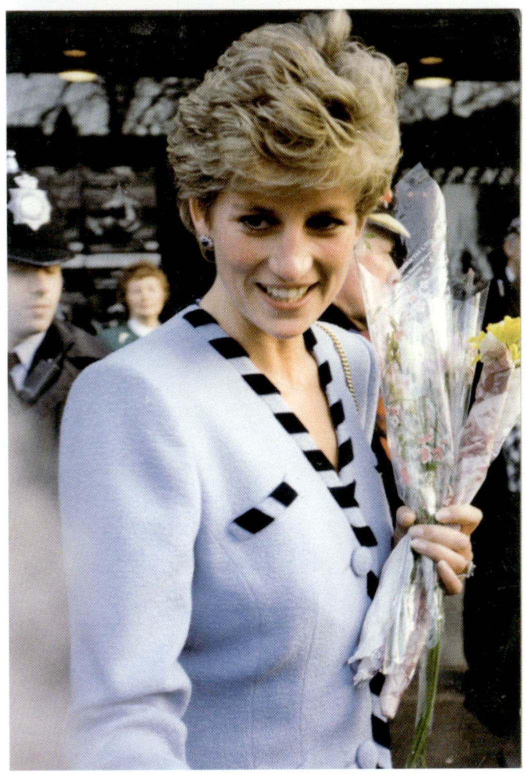

Princess Diana, Nottingham, 20 January 1993
With the announcement of her separation from the Prince, and the news full of Royal scandals, Princess Diana is back to work with a visit to Nottingham's Playhouse Theatre.

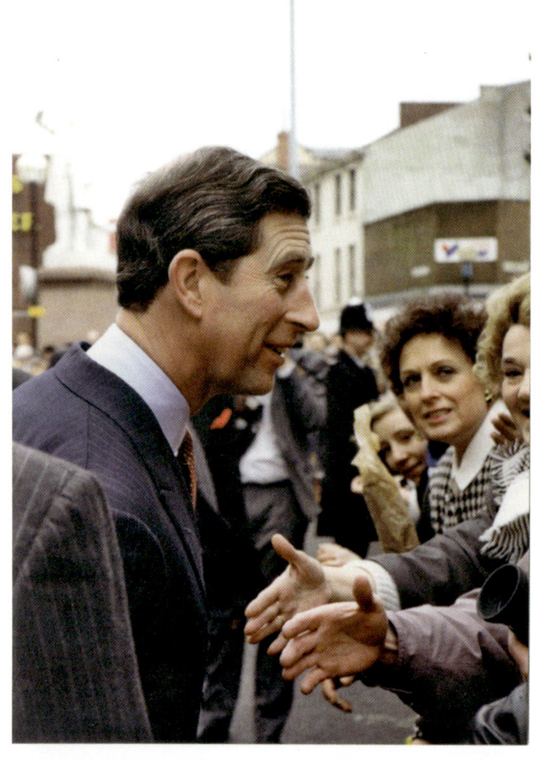

Prince Charles, Blackburn, 3 February 1993
Visiting St George's Hall in Blackburn, the Prince sees young entrepreneurs helped by his Prince's Youth Business Trust.

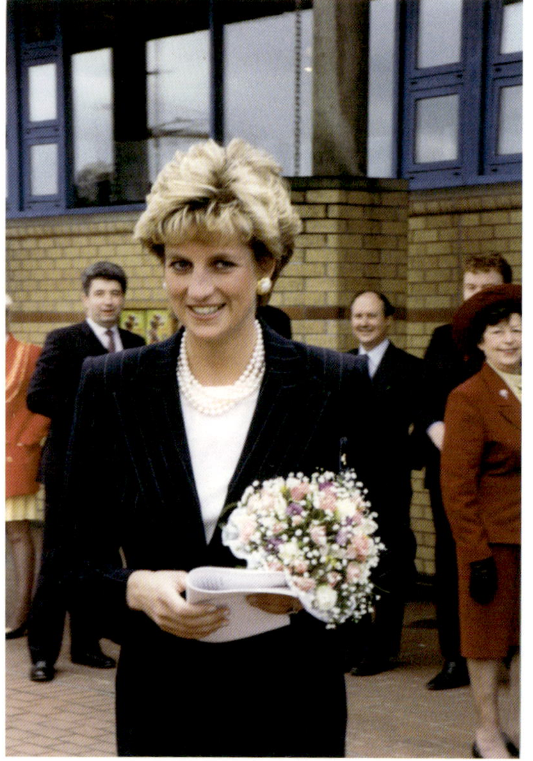

Princess Diana, Leeds, 6 April 1993
At the West Yorkshire Playhouse in Leeds, the Princess visited the 'Health of the Nation' conference organised by the Yorkshire Regional Health Authority. Outside, large crowds gathered. The previous month, whilst skiing with her children in Switzerland, press photographers had been troubling the Princess. 'Can I just say well done for sticking up to the photographers?' I said. 'Well, the boys are only ten and eight – and they needed protecting', she tenderly added.

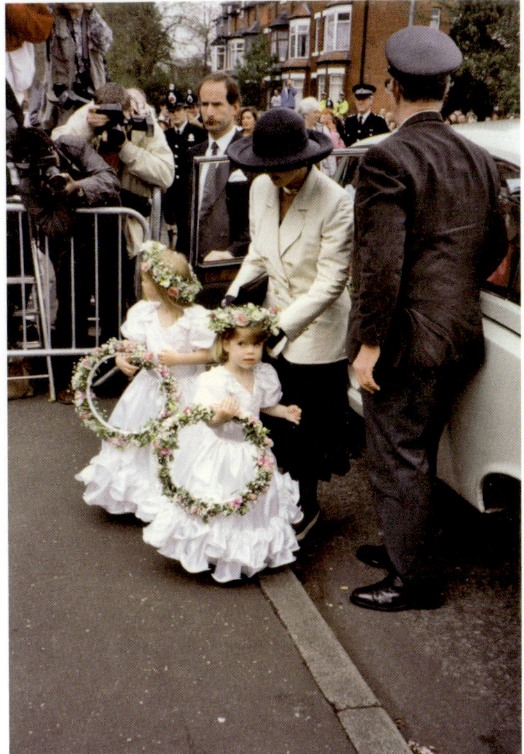

Sarah, Duchess of York and Princesses Beatrice and Eugenie, Manchester, 24 April 1993
St Chad's church, Manchester, was the location for the wedding of a Royal nanny, Alison Wardley. Her bridesmaids were her charges, the two young daughters of the Duke and Duchess of York, whose mother accompanied them for the day.

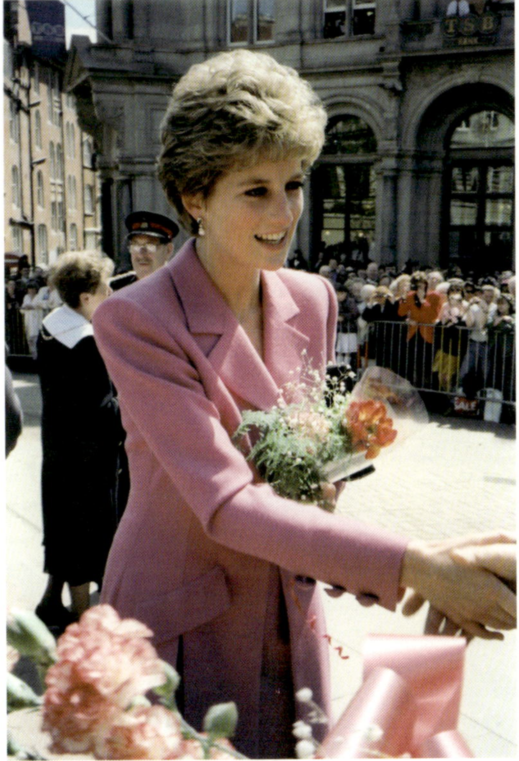

Princess Diana, Birmingham, 6 May 1993
Enormous crowds lined Victoria Square in Birmingham to welcome the Princess as she arrived to officially open the refurbished Square. She later went onto a fundraising lunch at the Metropole Hotel.

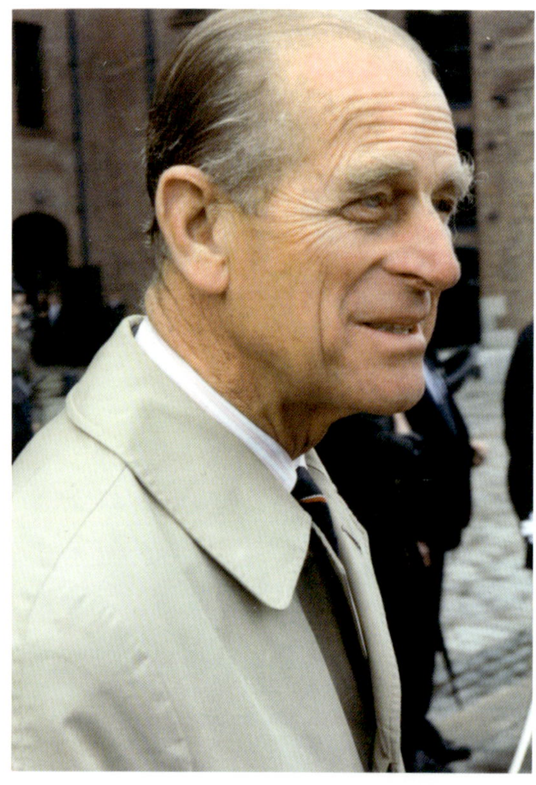

The Queen and the Duke of Edinburgh, Liverpool, 28 May 1993
Marking the fiftieth anniversary of the Battle of the Atlantic, the Queen and Prince Philip arrived at the Albert Dock, Liverpool, to large cheers, before visiting the National Maritime Museum.

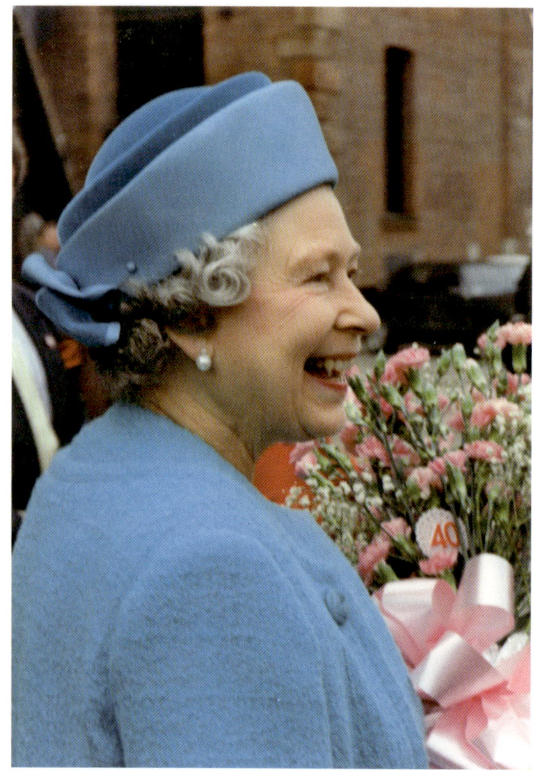

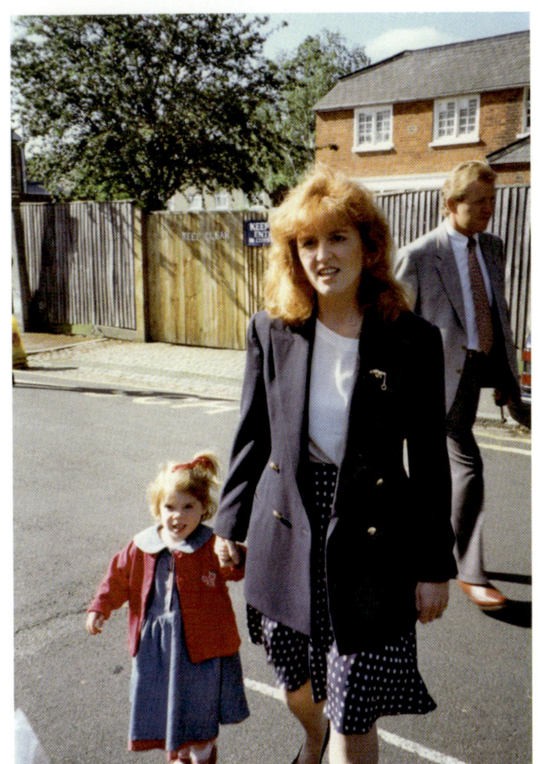

The Duchess of York with Princess Eugenie, Upton House School, Windsor, 15 June, 1993
The Royal Princesses attended a private school in Windsor, and the Duchess was always on hand to lend a cheery smile and wave to onlookers as she dropped them off each morning.

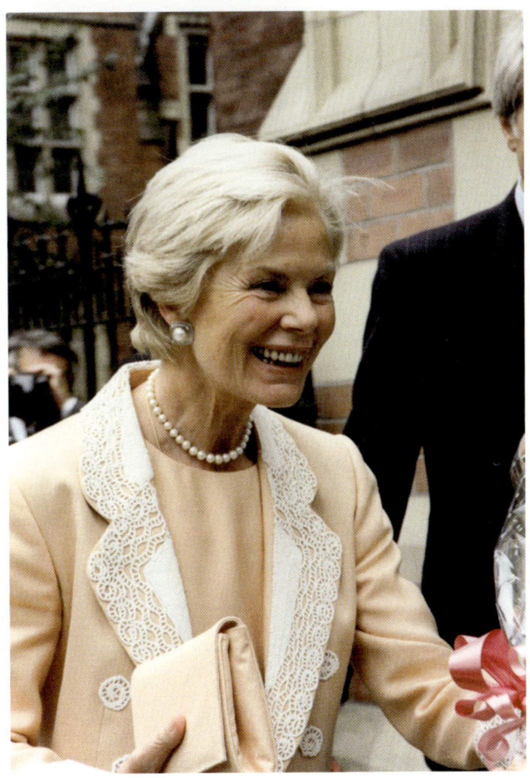

Katharine, Duchess of Kent, Leeds University, 27 July 1993
As Chancellor of the University of Leeds, the Duchess of Kent arrived to present the students' degrees.

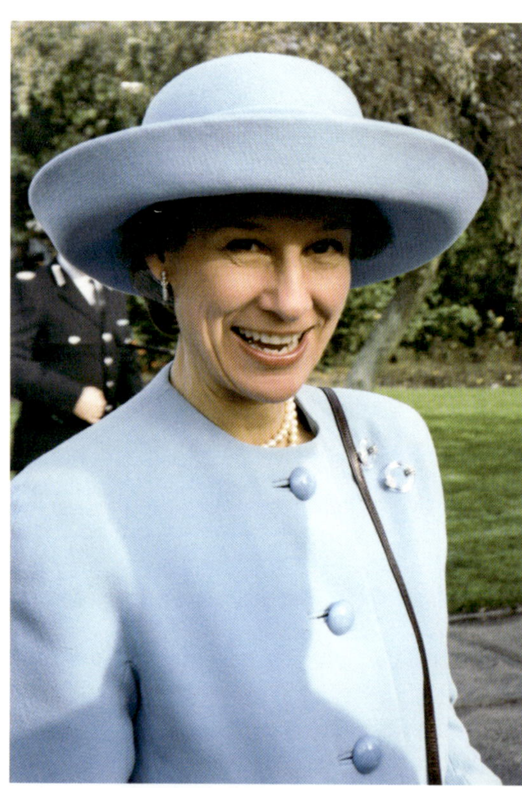

Left:
**The Duchess of Gloucester, Bury,
19 October 1993**
The Duchess of Gloucester visited the Minden
Medical Centre in Bury.

Below:
**Princess Diana, Manchester,
20 October 1993**
The Princess of Wales visited the Smithfield
Centre in Manchester to see the work of the
Guinness Trust. Sadly, the weather was less
than welcoming with rain!

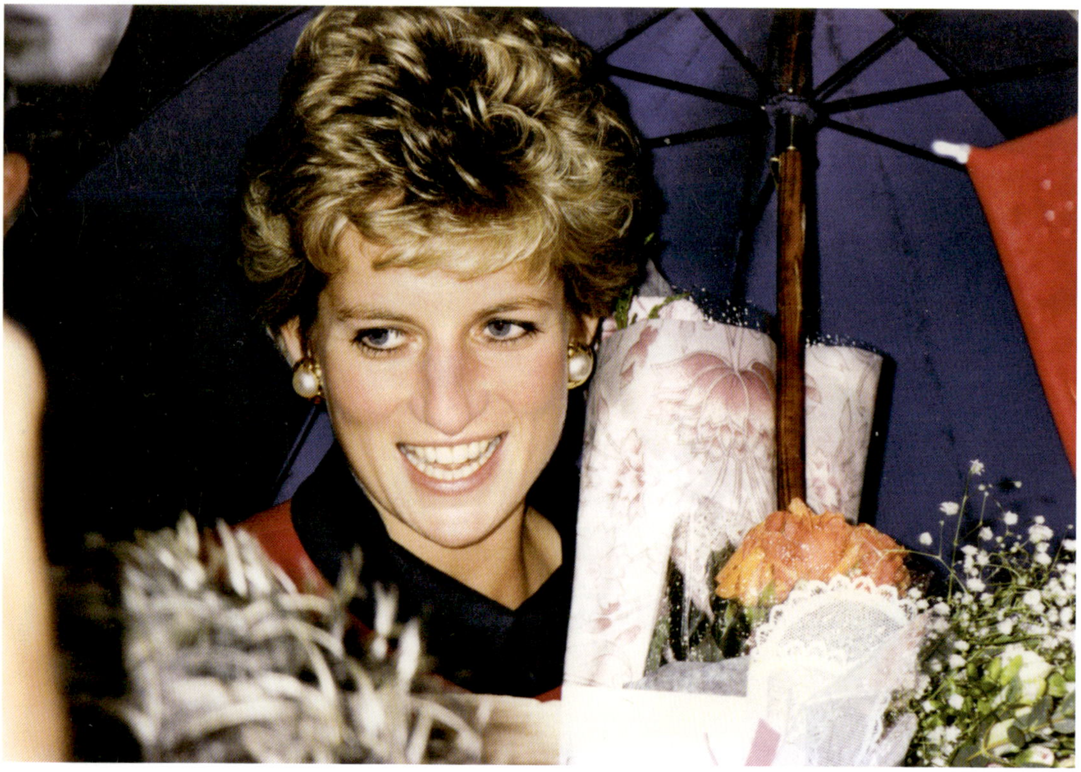

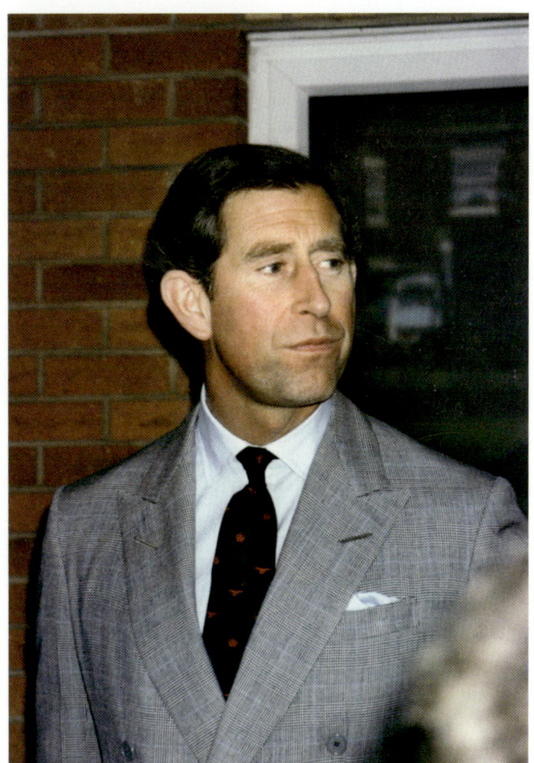

**Prince Charles, The Prince of Wales
Hospice, Pontefract, 17 November 1993**
The Prince of Wales visited the hospice that bears his name in Pontefract. On his arrival in the November sunshine, he greeted the crowds, and volunteers that had turned out to see him. 'It's so nice to see all the hard work achieves something', he added.

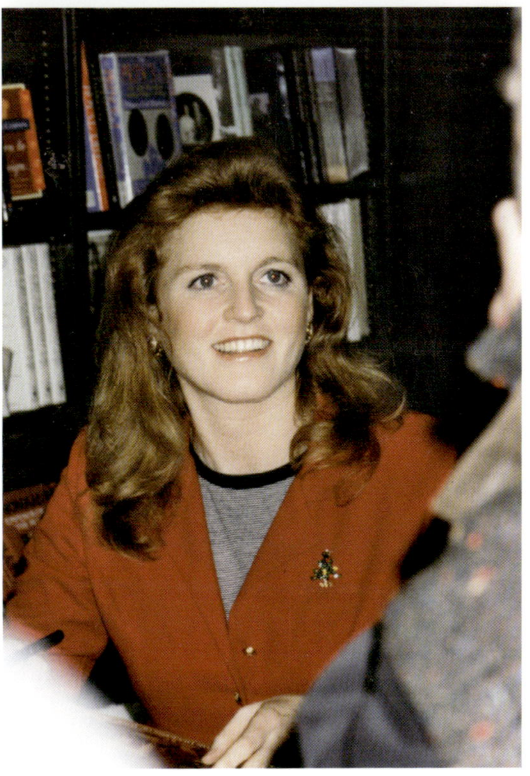

**The Duchess of York, London,
21 December 1993**
Promoting one of her books on Queen Victoria, the Duchess visited the famous Hatchards Bookshop in London's Piccadilly to sign copies.

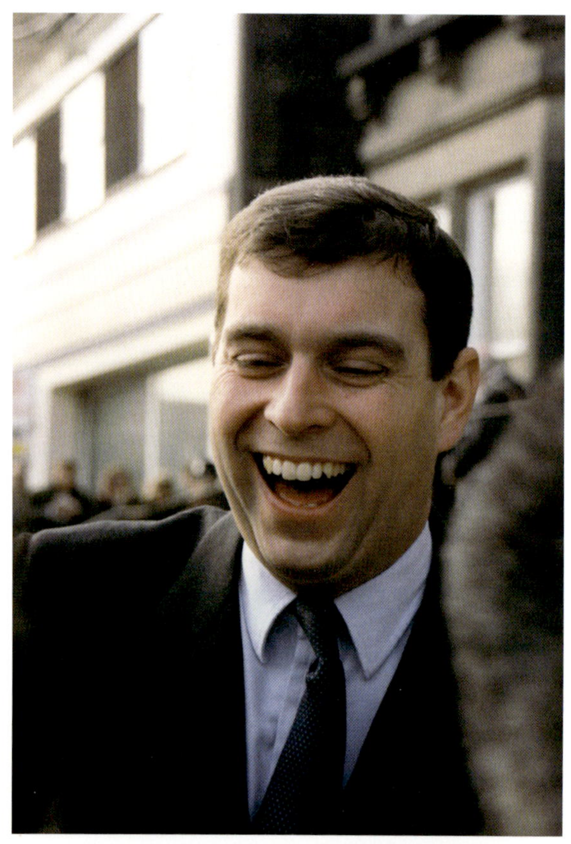

Left:
**Prince Andrew, Harrogate,
18 February 1994**
On the eve of his thirty-fourth birthday,
the Prince visited the new offices of the
Probation Service in Harrogate.

Below:
**Princess Margaret, Manchester,
12 April 1994**
Visiting St Margaret's church, and the
Youth Centre in Prestwich, Manchester,
the Princess found herself attracting
unwanted press attention as rumours
of her private life circulated the media.
Putting on a brave face, she went
ahead with her visit, marking the silver
anniversary of the club that she had
opened twenty-five years previously.

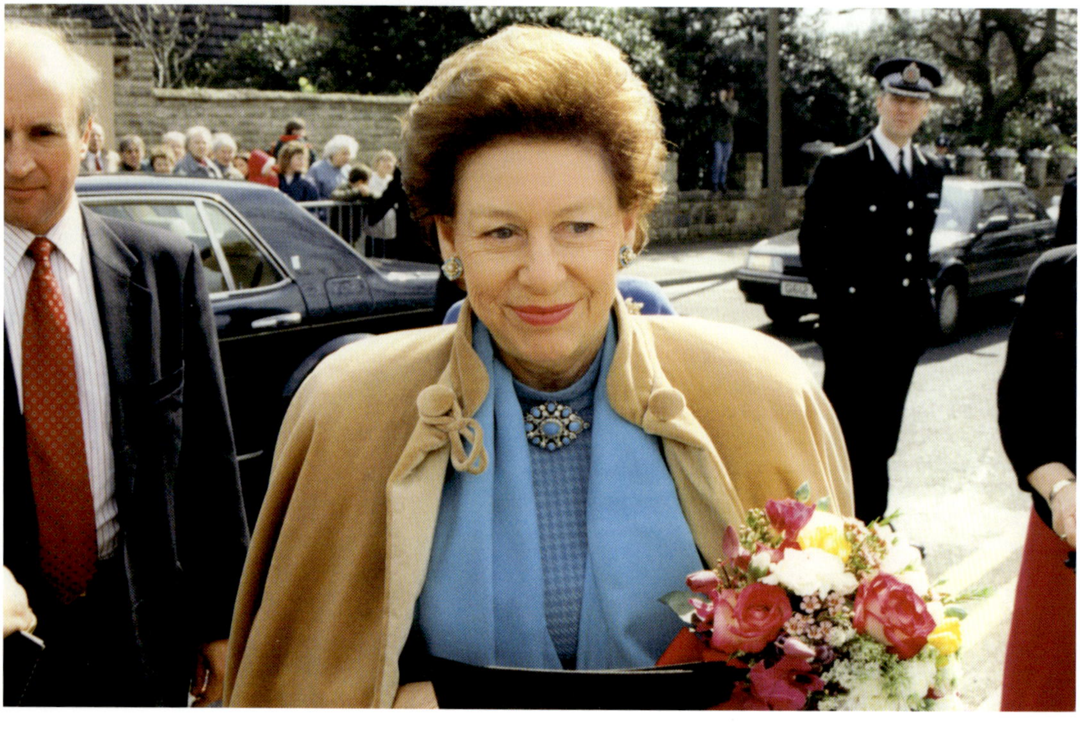

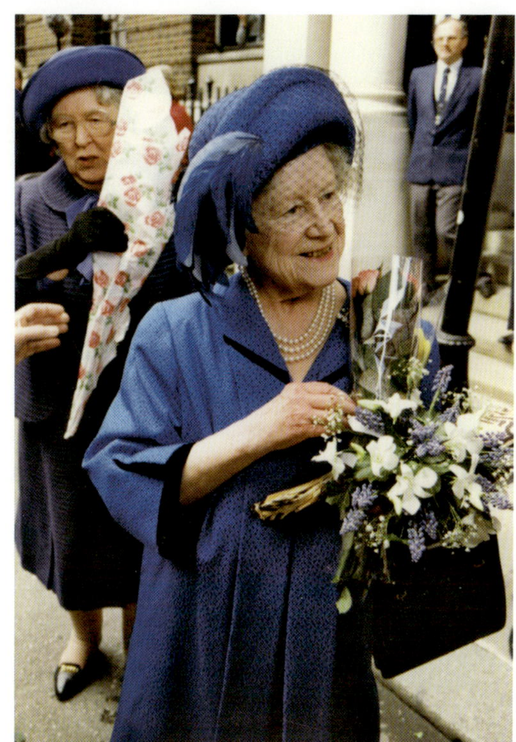

The Queen Mother, London, 13 April 1994
The Queen Mother visited St Mary's Hospital,
London to open the new Fleming Laboratories.

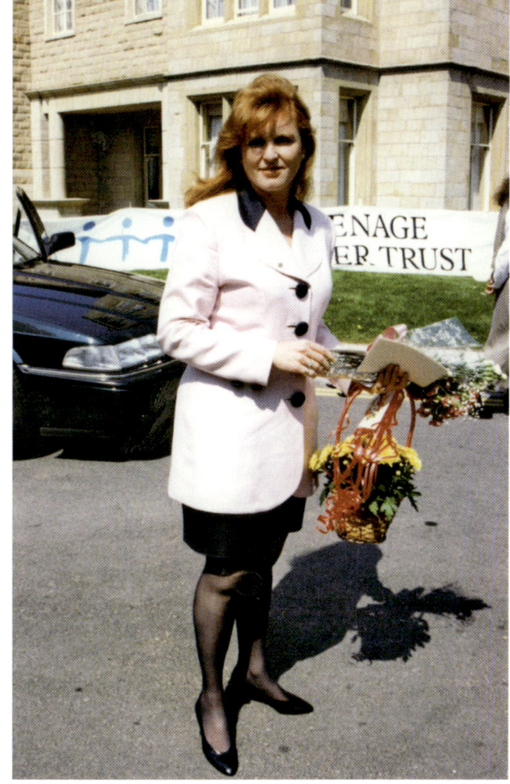

Sarah, Duchess of York, Leeds, 12 May 1994
Now officially separated, the Duchess visited
Leeds to see the International Conference on
Teenage Cancer, where she launched a campaign
to raise funds for the Teenage Cancer Trust to
build twenty specialist units. 'The sun's shining,
it was raining in London this morning when
I left', the Duchess remarked. Then, rather
candidly, she went on to say inside the building
she had an exchange of words with a reporter
who said she was doing this for her own image
– 'Well I said, if that's what you want to think ...'

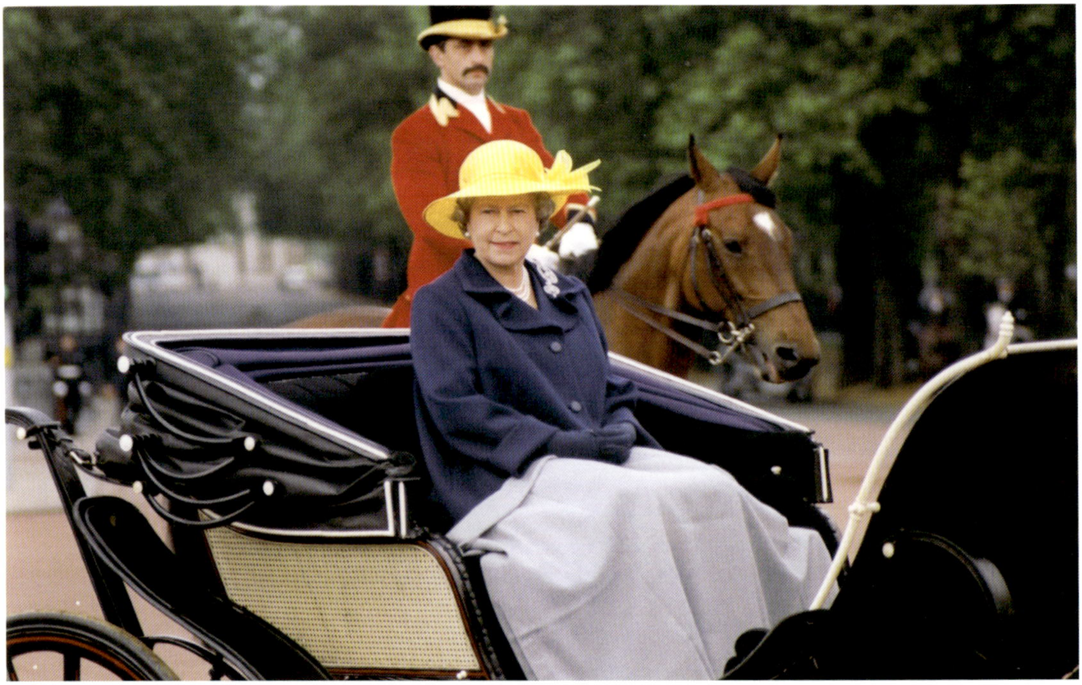

Trooping the Colour, London, 11 June 1994
Seated in her phaeton, once used by Queen Victoria, the Queen travelled down The Mall to watch her official birthday parade, and later joined members of her family for the traditional balcony appearance at Buckingham Palace.

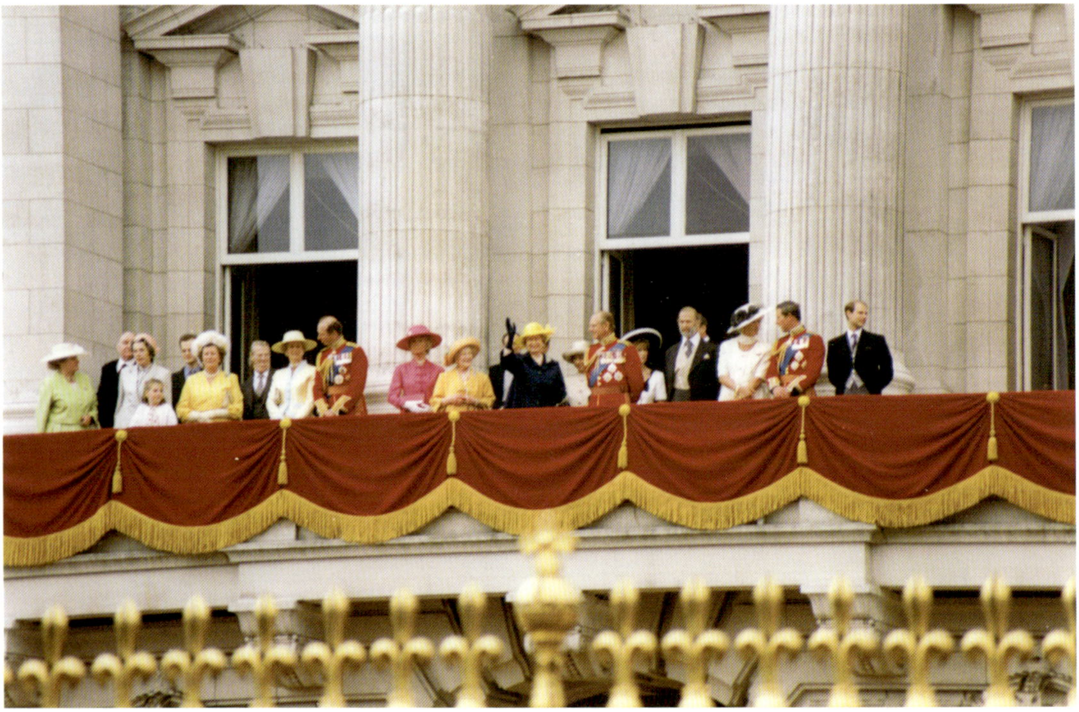

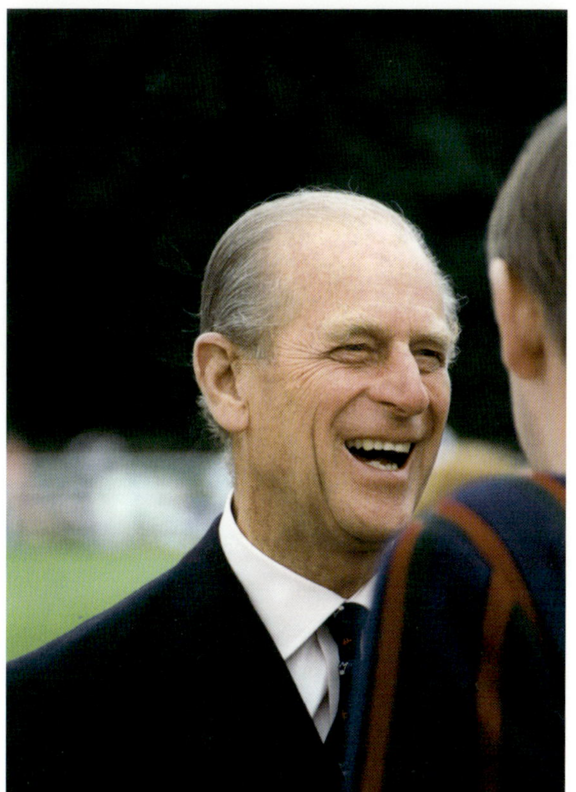

Princes Philip and Edward, Windsor, 12 June 1994

Alongside his son Edward, Prince Philip attended as Trustee of the Prince Phillip Fund for the Royal Borough of Windsor and Maidenhead, and as Twelfth Man of the Lord's Taverners, for a charity cricket match held in the grounds of Windsor Great Park, with the castle as its backdrop.

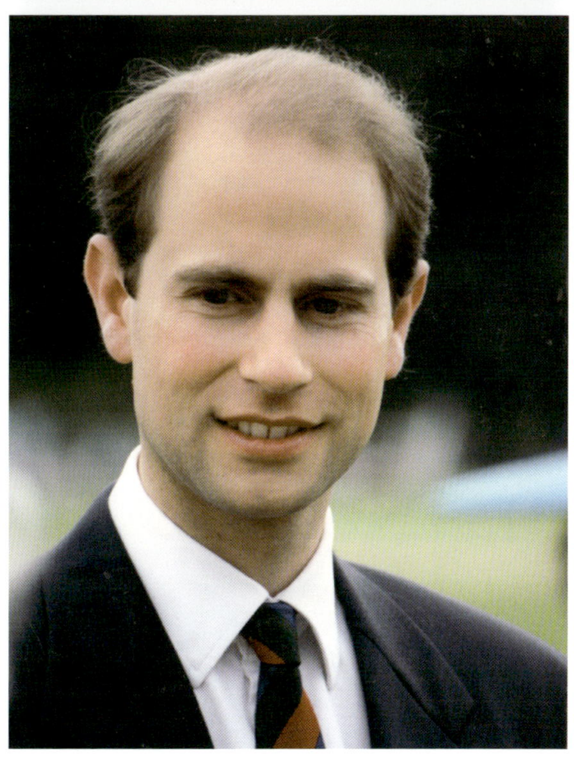

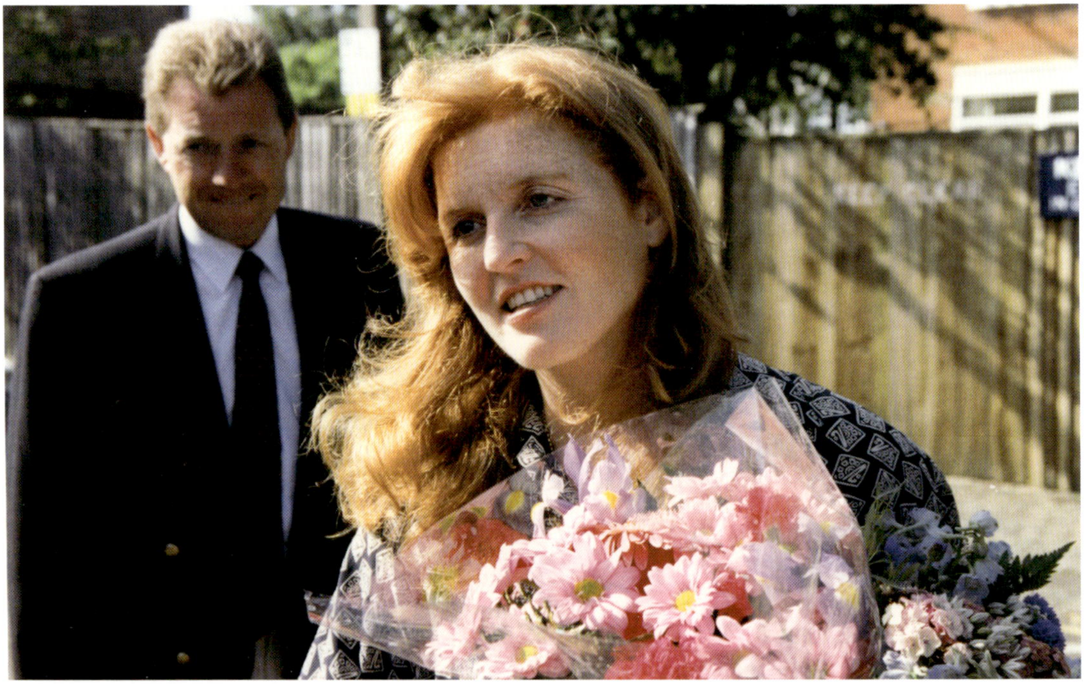

The Duchess of York, Windsor, 14 June 1994
Dropping off her children at Upton House School, minutes away from Windsor town centre, the Duchess of York accepted flowers from well-wishers.

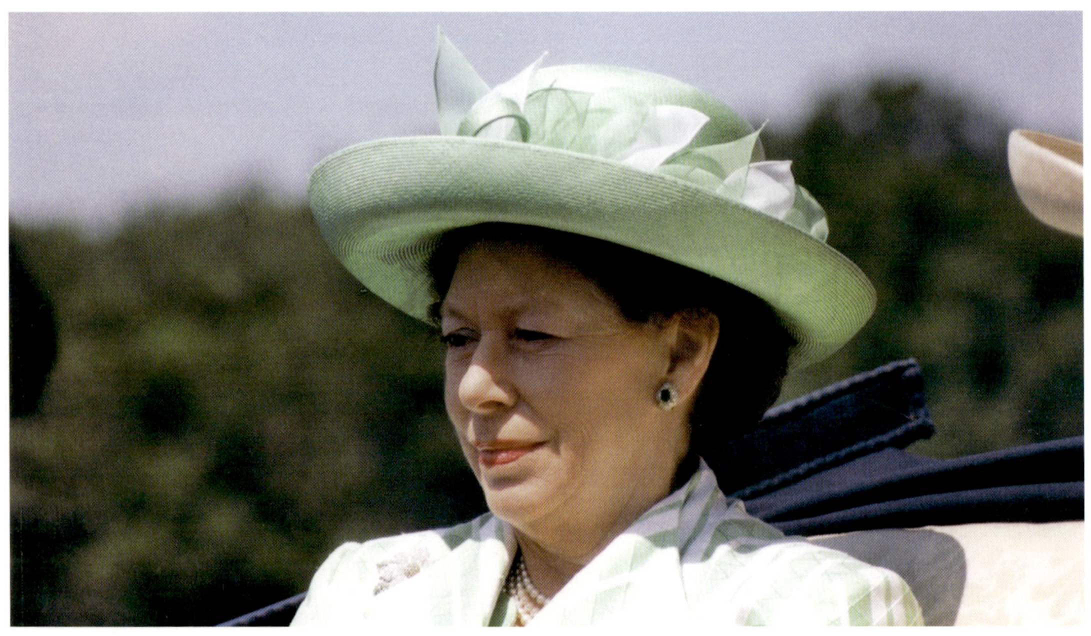

Princess Margaret, Royal Ascot, 14 June 1994
Princess Margaret (below) and the Queen Mother (opposite) were the two Royal ladies on show at this year's race meeting, wearing their finest outfits and hats.

Right:
The Queen Mother, Royal Ascot, 15 June 1994
Royal Ascot was always a time that the Queen
Mother looked forward to. Her love of horse
racing was very much in evidence.

Below:
The Queen, Wolverhampton, 24 June 1994
The Queen attended a service to mark
the foundation of St Peter's church,
Wolverhampton, during her visit to the region.
As she walked though St Peter's Square in the
hot sunshine, she met the crowds.

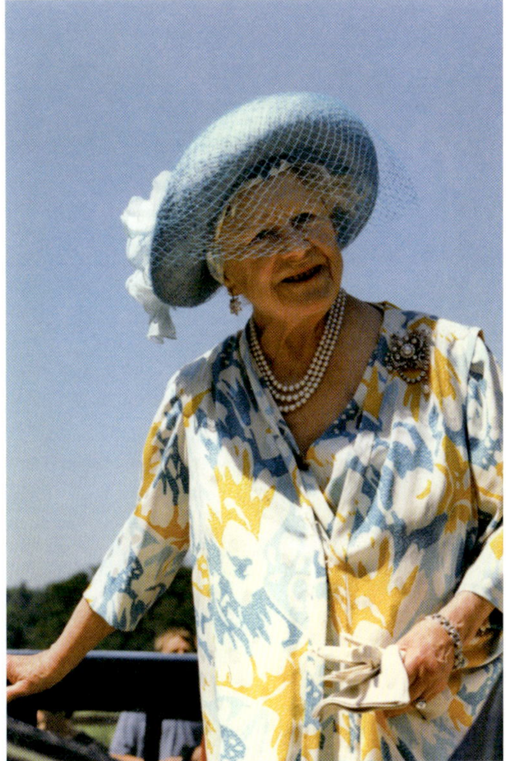

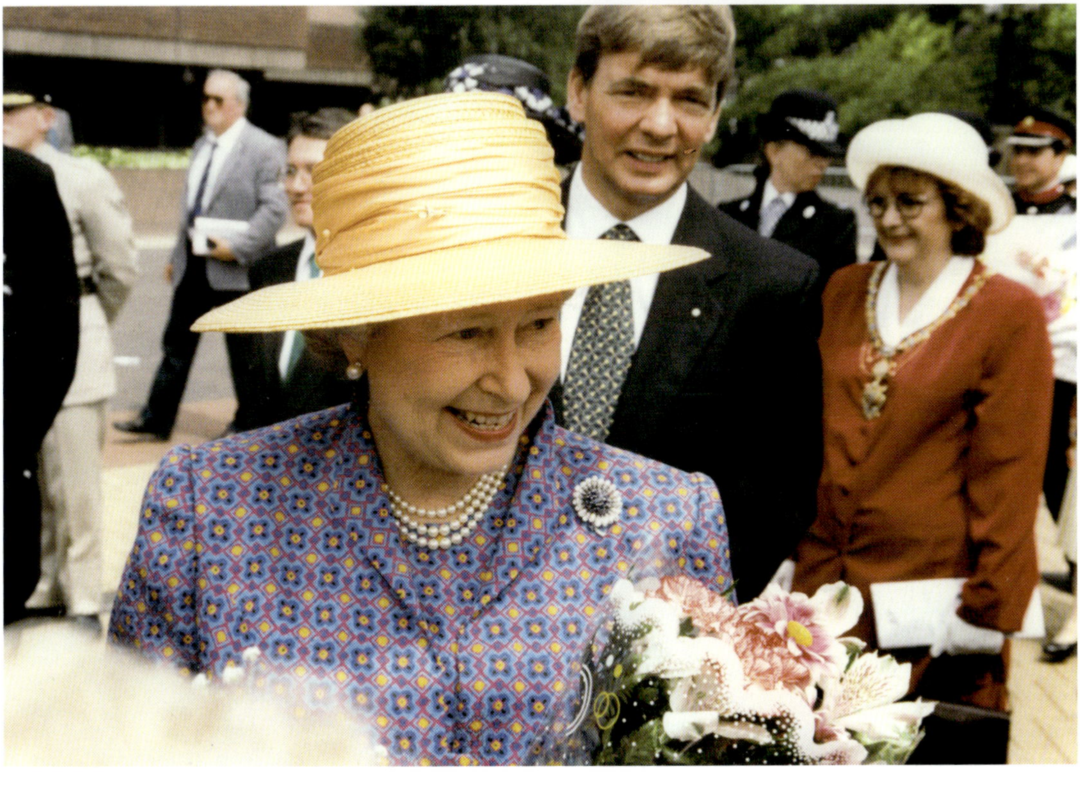

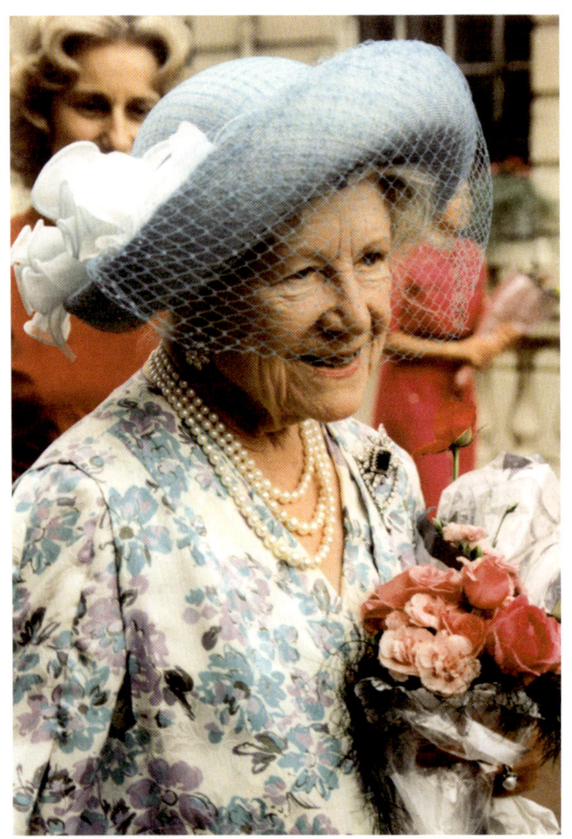

The Queen Mother's 94th birthday, London, 4 August 1994

In what became a tradition in the Royal calendar, the Queen Mother met the crowds of well-wishers who had gathered outside the gates of her London home, Clarence House. Many of them had camped overnight to ensure a good position. The highlight for all was the appearance of the Royal Family alongside her (below). Here the young Princes William and Harry stand next to their grandmother's page, William Tallon.

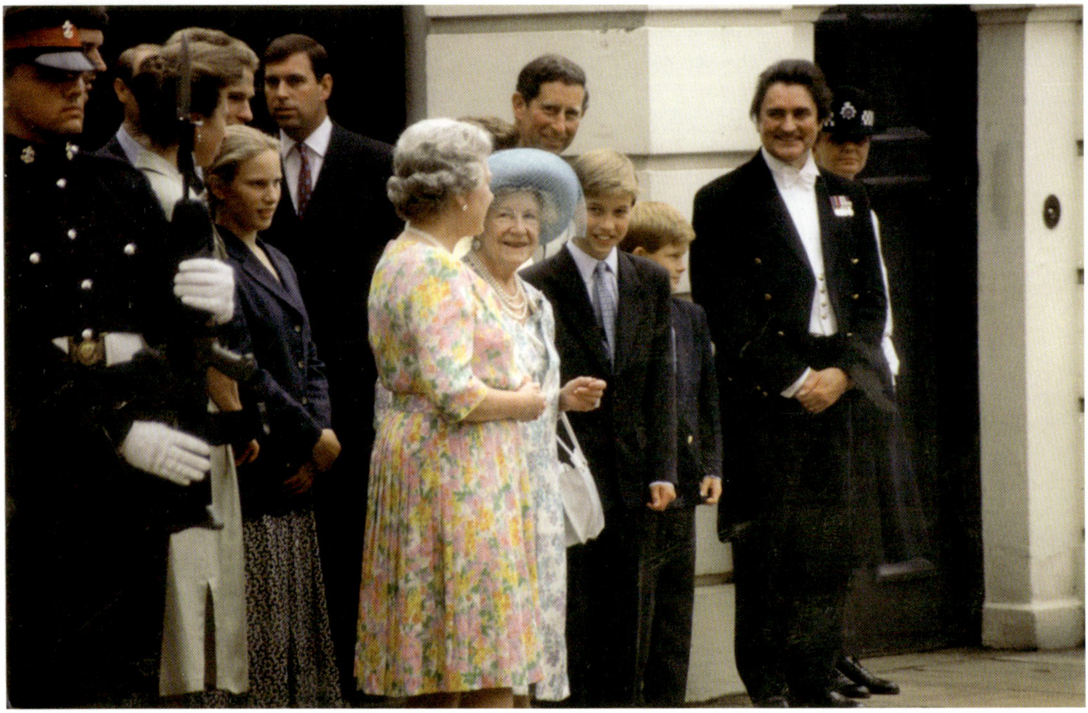

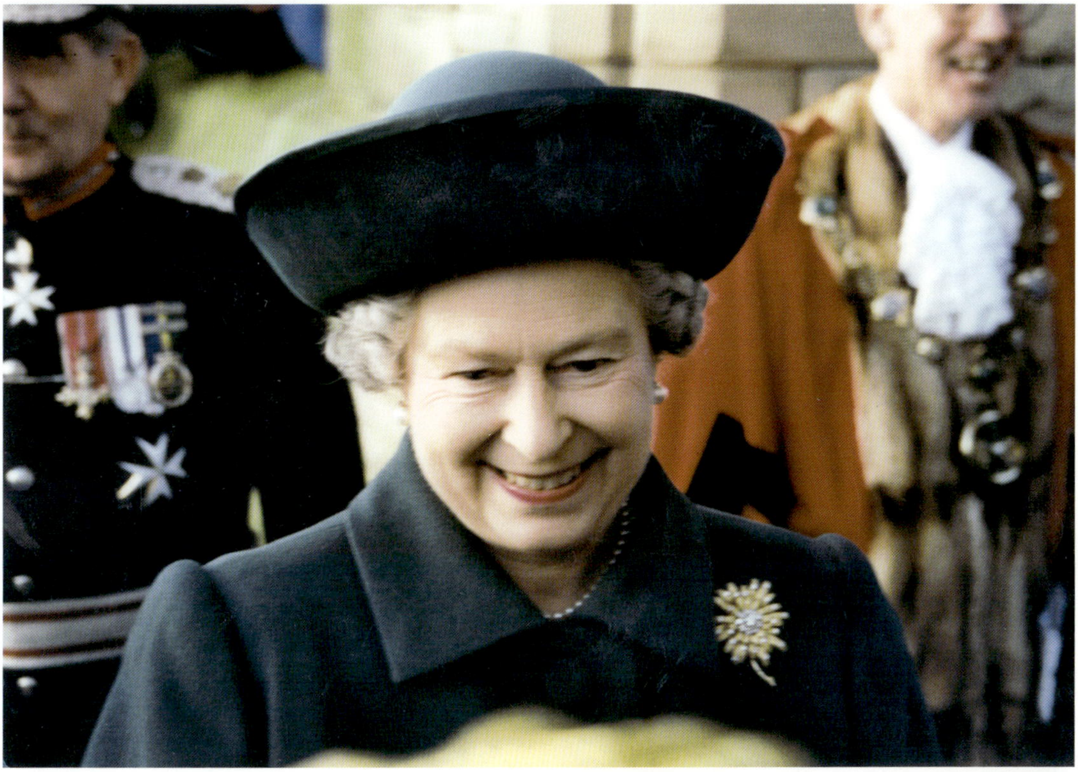

Her Majesty The Queen, Rochdale,
1 December 1994

After arriving at the railway station, the Queen attended a service at Rochdale's parish church to mark its 800th anniversary.

Her Majesty The Queen, West Newton,
5 February 1995

When she stays at Sandringham, in Norfolk, the Queen likes to attend church every Sunday, and also alternates between churches on the estate. Here she attended Morning Service on the last Sunday of her six-week stay at St Peter and St Paul church in the village of West Newton. After the service, she walked up to the Church Hall to present Bibles to children to mark good attendance at school.

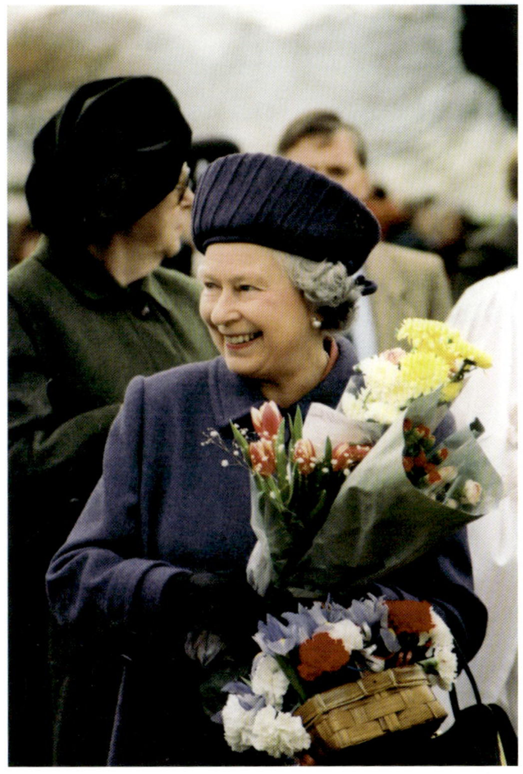

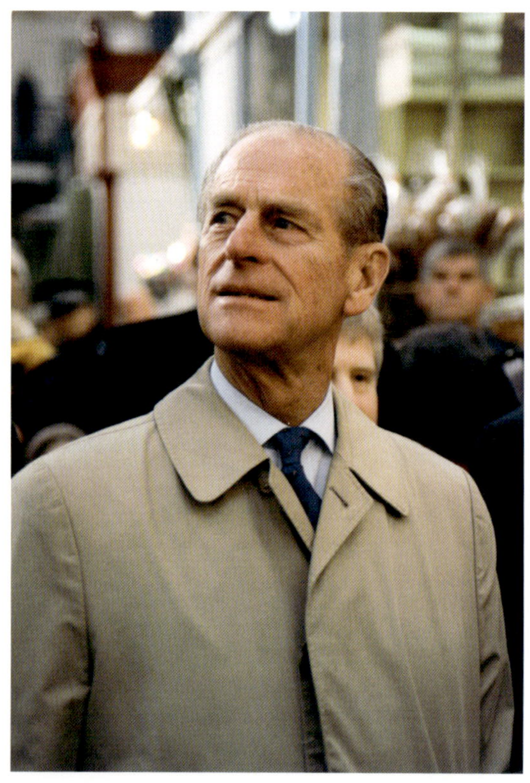

The Duke of Edinburgh, Kirkgate Market, Leeds, 17 February 1995

Prince Philip visited Leeds Kirkgate Market to see the £8 million refurbishment, and meet traders and shoppers. His mischievous side was in play that day as he said to one lady shopper, pointing towards a baker's, 'Those are big sandwiches don't you think?', and when he turned to the lady Lord Mayor as they passed a clothing stall, he pointed to a rather revealing nightie and commented, 'Is this the sort of thing you wear then ..?' with a twinkle in his eye.

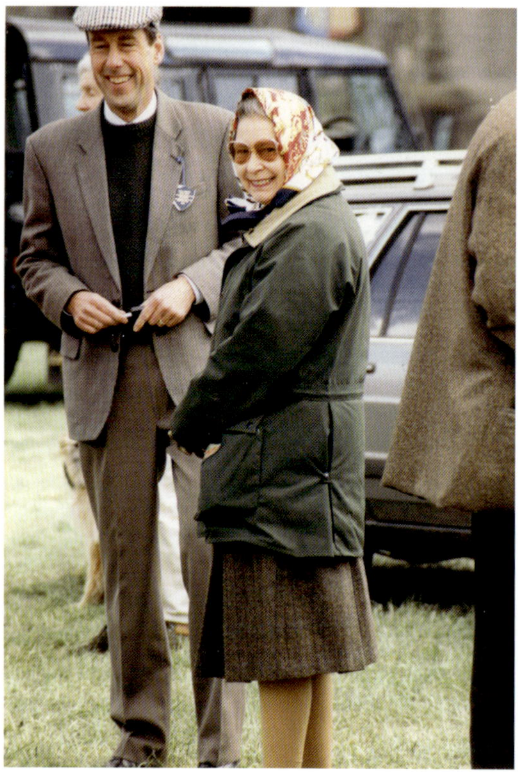

The Royal Windsor Horse Show, 13 May 1995

Here's an opportunity to see the Queen as very few do, relaxed and informal. At the Royal Windsor Horse Show, held annually in the grounds of the Castle, she walks around, her Hermès headscarf and wax jacket the order of the day. While her son Prince Edward rode around on his horse, her cousin, Prince Michael of Kent, rode alongside Princess Irene of Hesse in the Concours d'Elegance.

Right:
Prince Edward at the Royal Windsor Horse Show, 13 May 1995
Many members of the Royal family are accomplished horse riders.

Below:
Prince Michael of Kent at the Royal Windsor Horse Show, 14 May 1995
It looks to be a very dull May day, as the passengers appear to be dressed in warm winter coats.

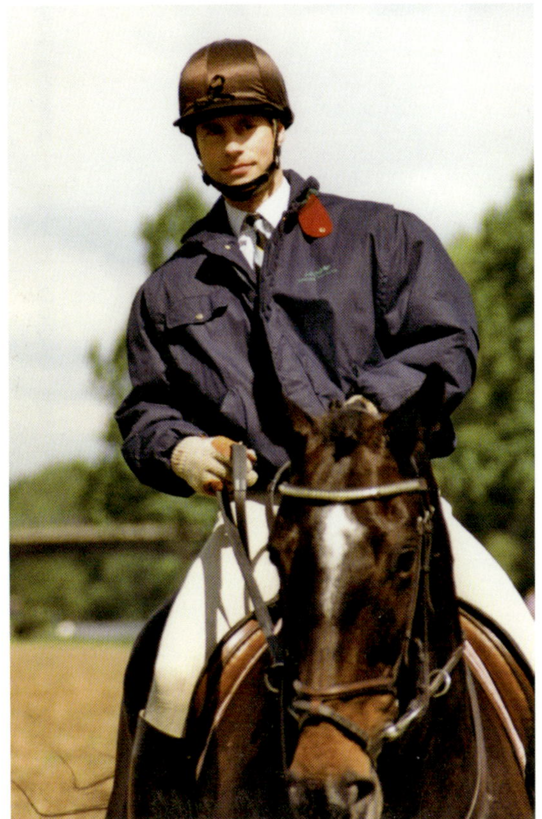

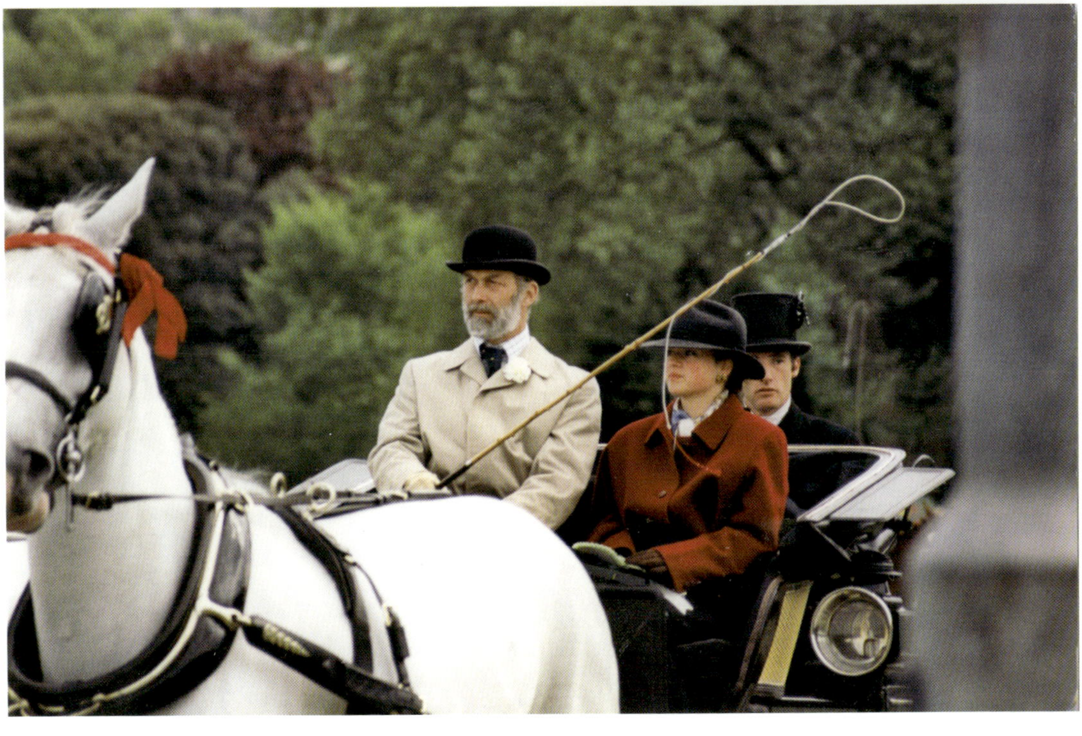

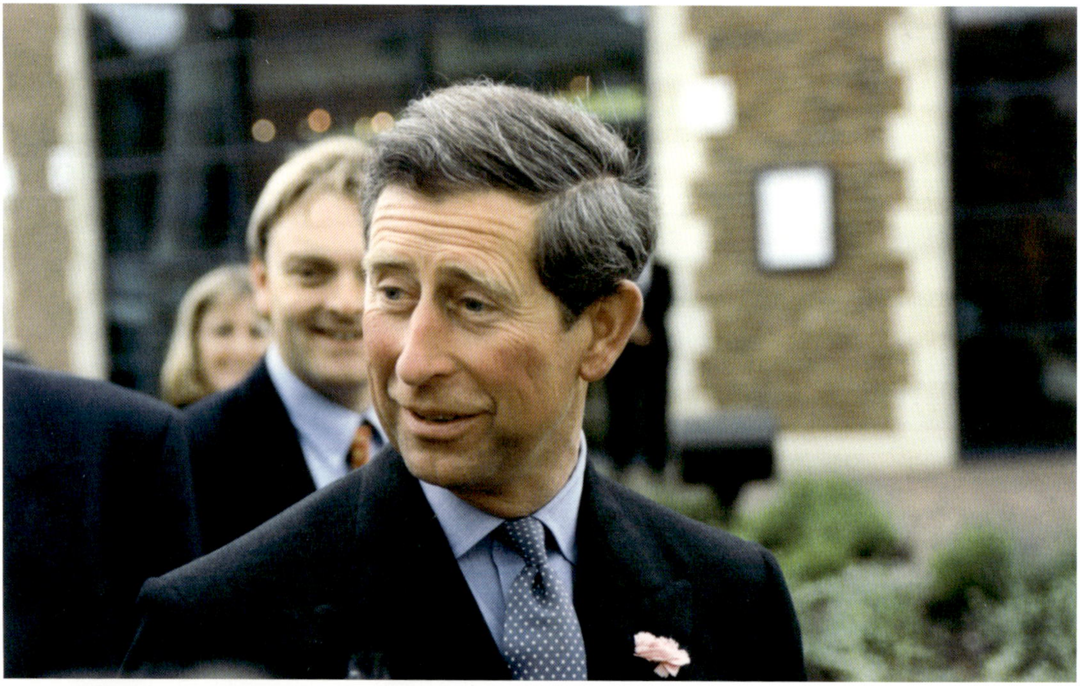

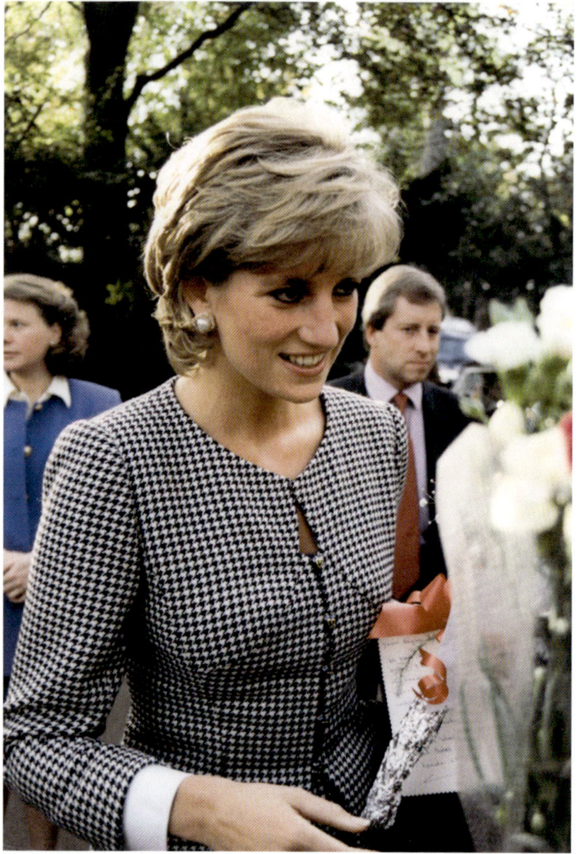

Prince Charles, Leeds, 9 June 1995
Visiting the Tetley's Brewery Wharf complex in Leeds, Prince Charles was there to meet young people starting out in business, and those who had benefited from the help of his Trust. 'Are you going in for a drink?' he joked before leaving.

Left:

Princess Diana, Birmingham, 31 October 1995
This was the last time I photographed the Princess, and the memories of the day are very special as she was on great form and extremely happy. Here she walks through the crowds after her visit to the Foundation for Conductive Education in Birmingham. The Princess cheekily turned to some officer cadets and said, 'So what are we up to today then boys?'

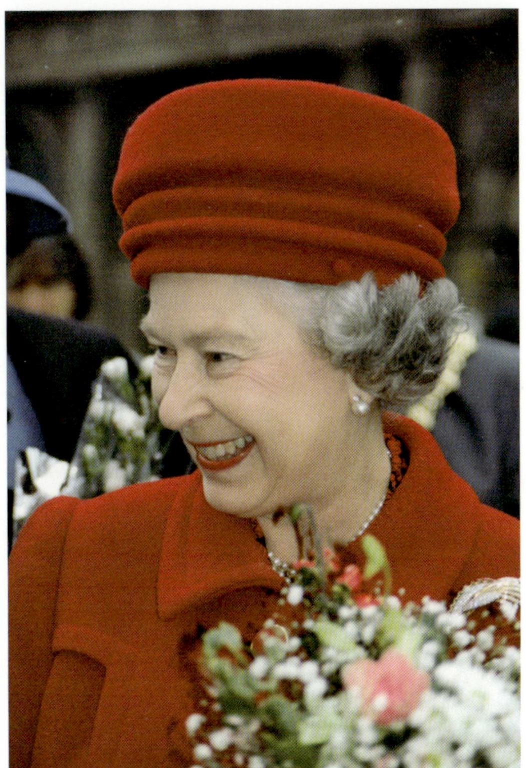

The Queen, Stoke-on-Trent, 7 December 1995
The Queen arrived on a snowy day at Stoke-on-Trent's railway station, and charmed the crowds, looking very festive in a red coat and hat. I passed on a card for the Queen Mother, who had a recent health scare. 'Oh, she's coming on rather well', the Queen replied.

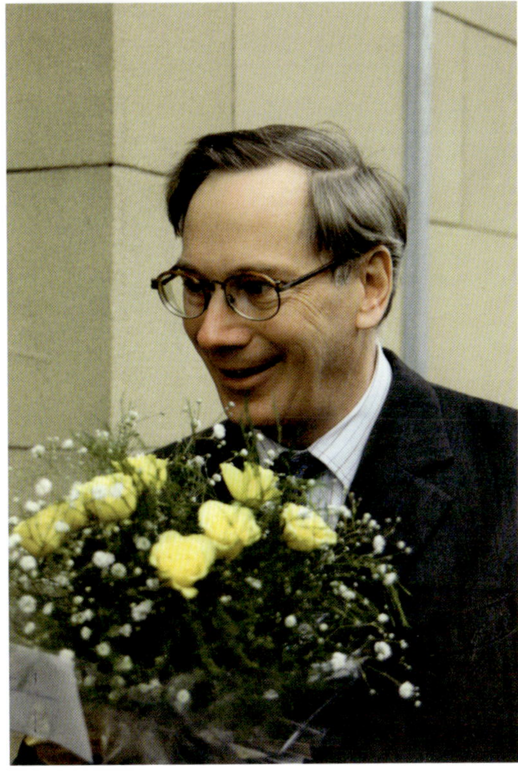

The Duke of Gloucester, Macclesfield, 7 December 1995
Later that same day, the Queen's cousin, the Duke of Gloucester, opened the new extension to the Cheshire Building Society in Macclesfield, and accepted a beautiful bouquet of yellow roses for the visit.

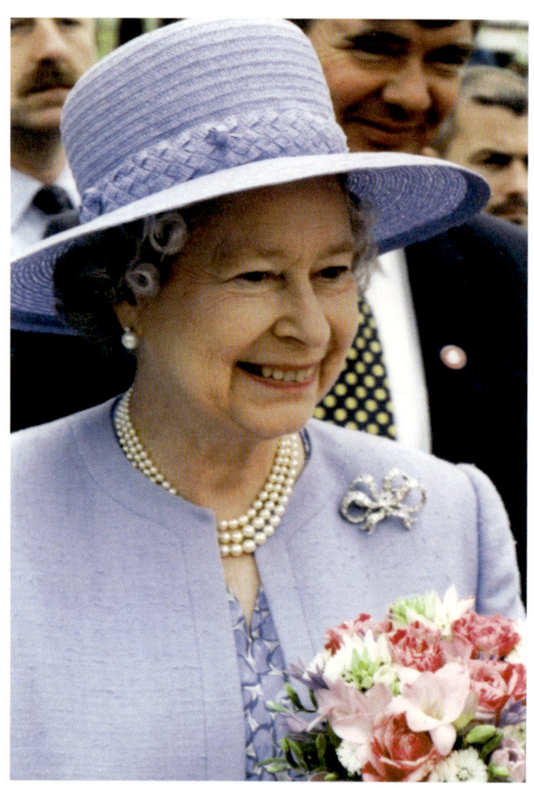

Left:
The Queen, Birkenhead, 7 June 1996
The Queen visited Birkenhead to visit Europa Square. Earlier in the day she had visited Sir Paul McCartney's FAME school in the city, and then it was back into Liverpool to watch a performance by the Philharmonic Orchestra.

Below:
Princess Alexandra of Kent, Leeds, 18 May 1998
Princess Alexandra visited the British Red Cross Society's new Northern Regional Office in Headingley. In her role as president, she visits as many of the charity's fundraising schemes as possible.

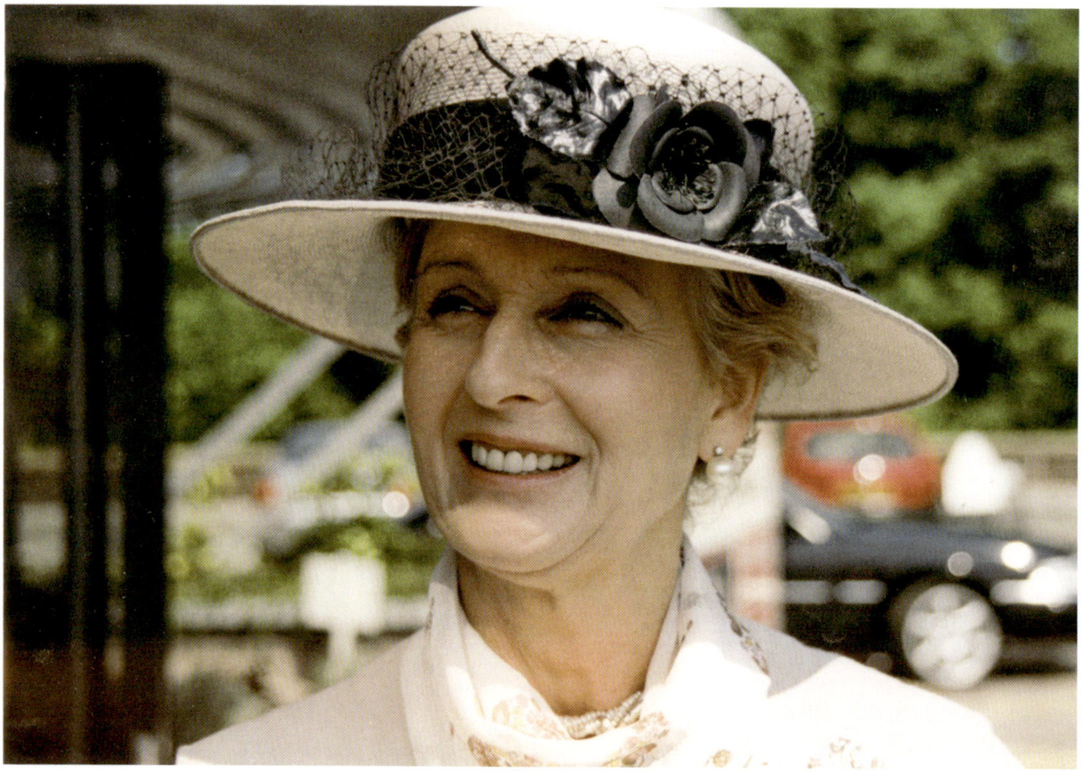

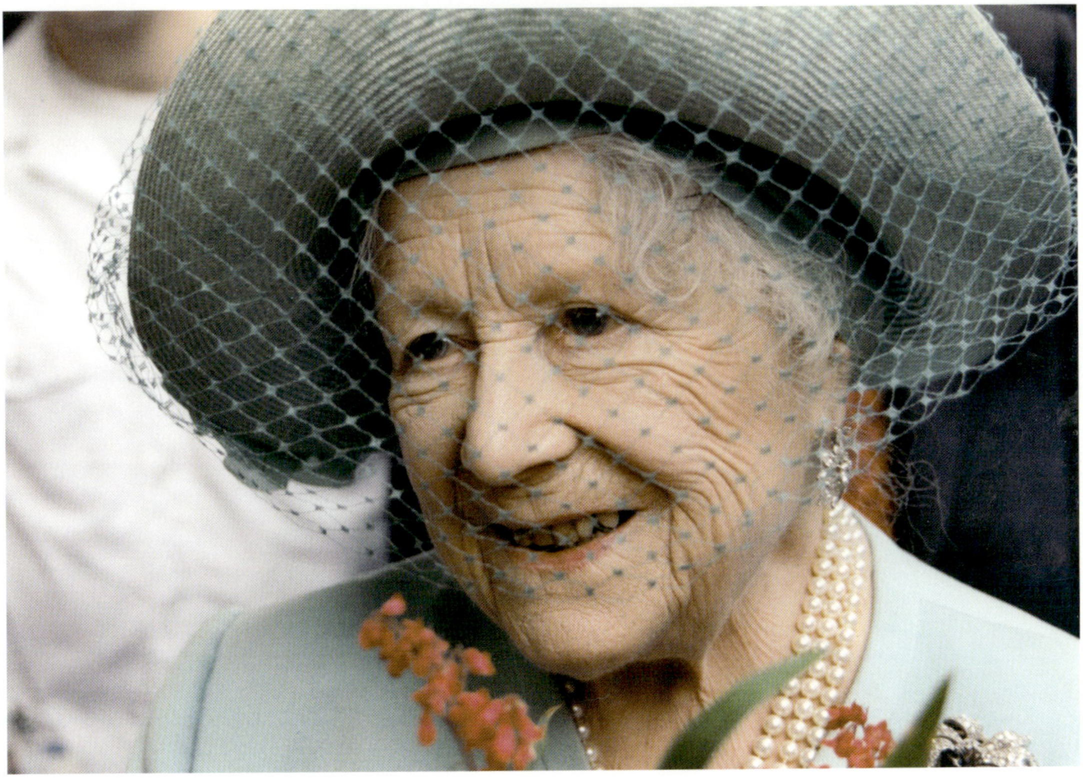

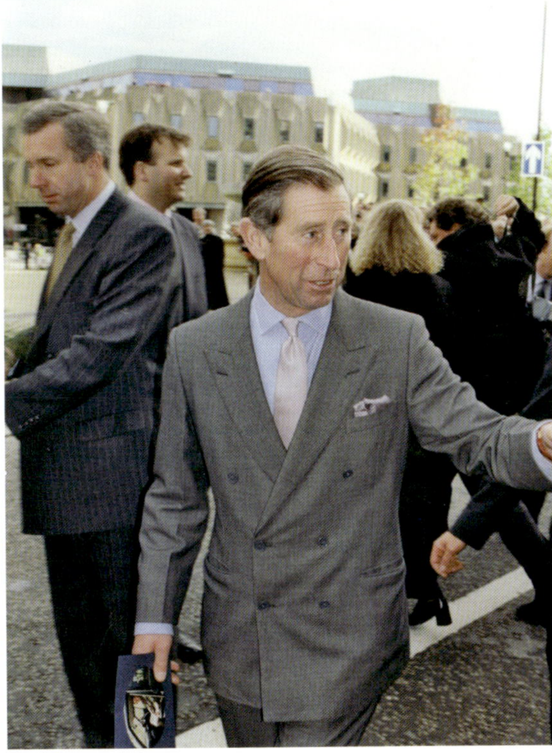

The Queen Mother, St Mary's Hospital, Paddington, London, 4 June 1998
The Queen Mother came once again to St Mary's Hospital, London, to unveil a plaque to mark the laying of the Foundation Stone of the Paediatric Accident and Emergency Centre.

Right:

Prince Charles, Sheffield, 14 November 1998
On the eve of his fiftieth birthday, Prince Charles chose to spend the day in Sheffield. After visiting the Town Hall to see the 'Heart of the City' Project and inspect the new Peace Gardens, the Prince mingled with well-wishers. Many of them gave him birthday cards, balloons and cakes!

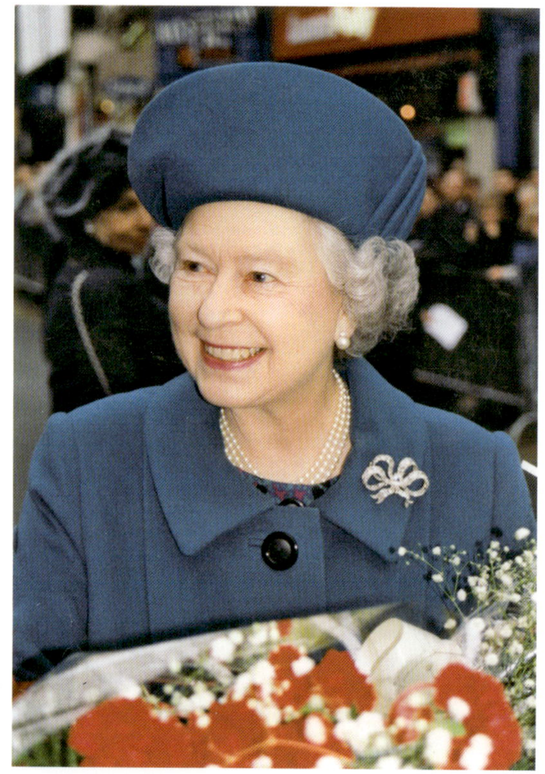

The Queen, Harrogate, 10 December 1998
The Queen came to Harrogate to visit its theatre, prior to the run up to Christmas. Outside, on the town's Oxford Street, excited shoppers and schoolchildren had gathered to see her.

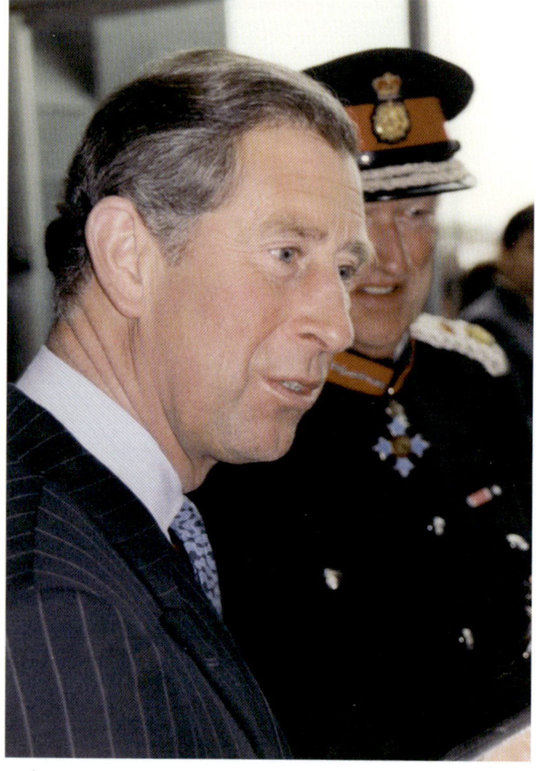

Prince Charles, Leeds, 16 April 1999
As Patron of Breakthrough Breast Cancer, Prince Charles visited the Royal Armouries, Leeds to launch the 'Breakthrough Corporate Challenge'.

The Duchess of Gloucester, Harrogate, April 1999

The Duchess of Gloucester visited Harrogate's International Centre to attend the BLISS (Baby Life Support Systems) Third International Neo-Natal Conference. She referred rather touchingly to her aged mother-in-law, Princess Alice, by saying 'She's a little frail now, but we see her every day.'

Below:

The Duchess of York, Asda, Pudsey, Leeds, 7 June 1999

The Duchess played the part of a checkout operator during a visit to Asda's Pudsey supermarket. Officially there to promote one of the many charities she is involved with, 'Tommy's Campaign', she couldn't resist the chance to ring up the sale of a pin badge to one little girl. 'I'm a woman of the '90s', she declared outside to me. Inside, she went on to receive a cheque from Asda's employees and then read excerpts of her Budgie books to local children. 'I hope you're not taking photos up my skirt', she joked to the press!

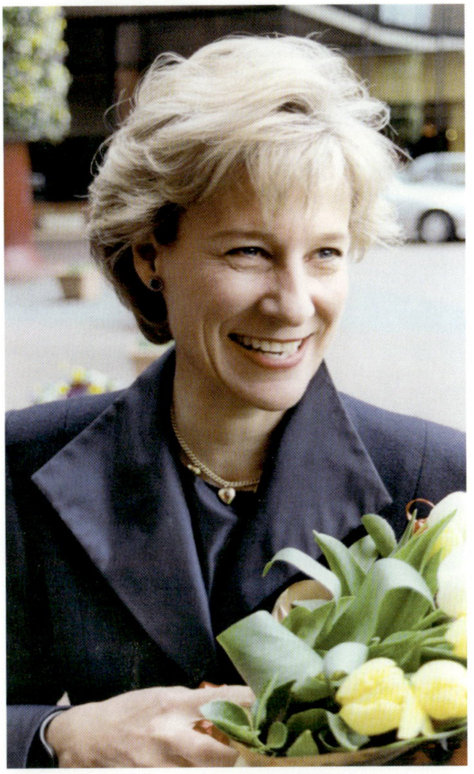

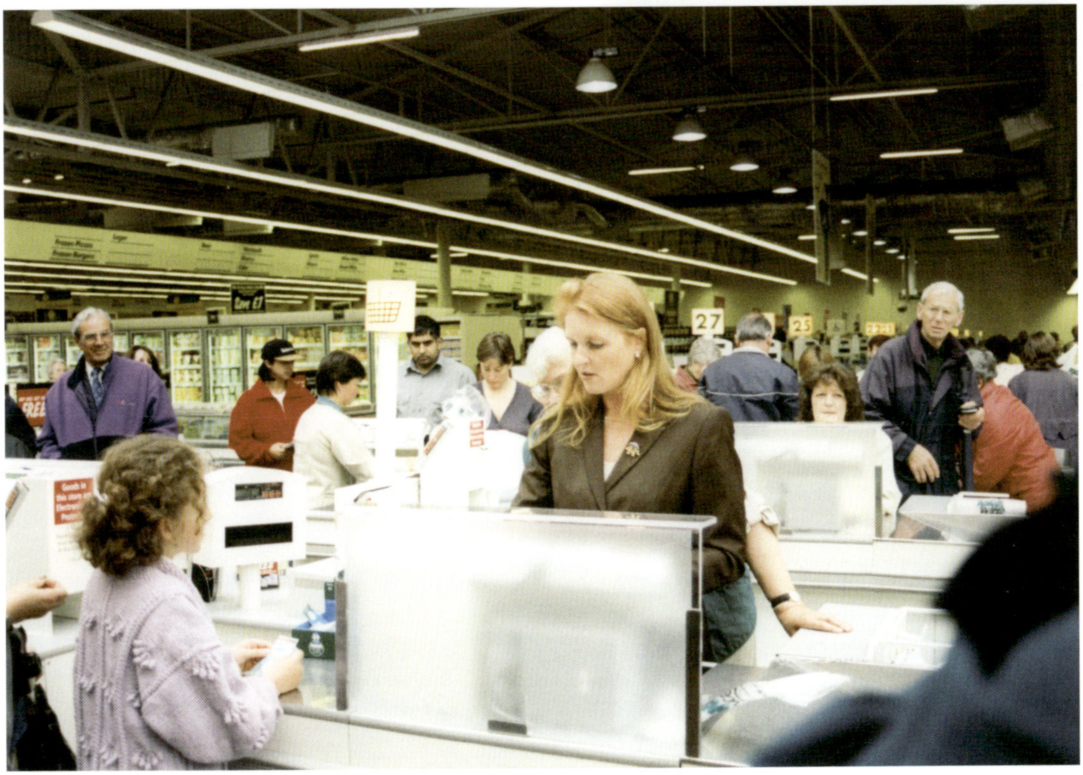

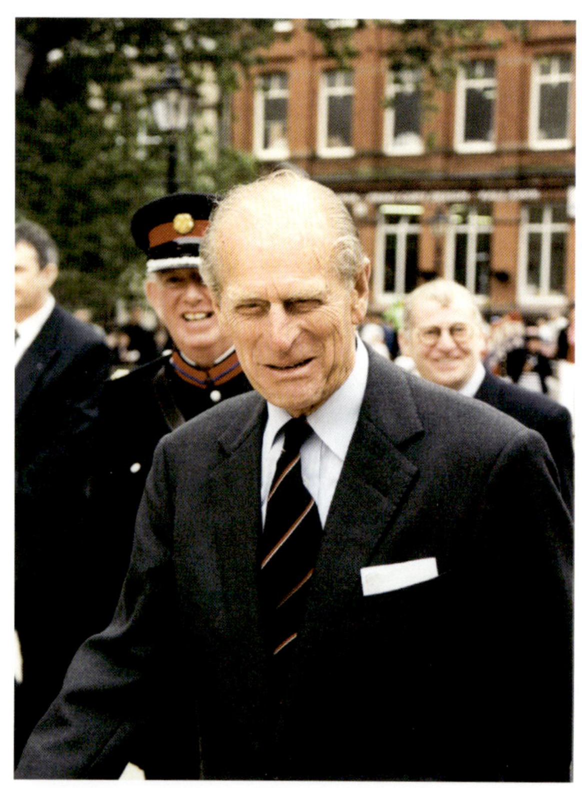

The Queen and the Duke of Edinburgh, Hull, 4 June 1999
Celebrating the 700th anniversary of the City of Hull, the Queen and Prince attended a special service at the Holy Trinity church. Both she and the Prince seemed genuinely delighted with the reception they received.

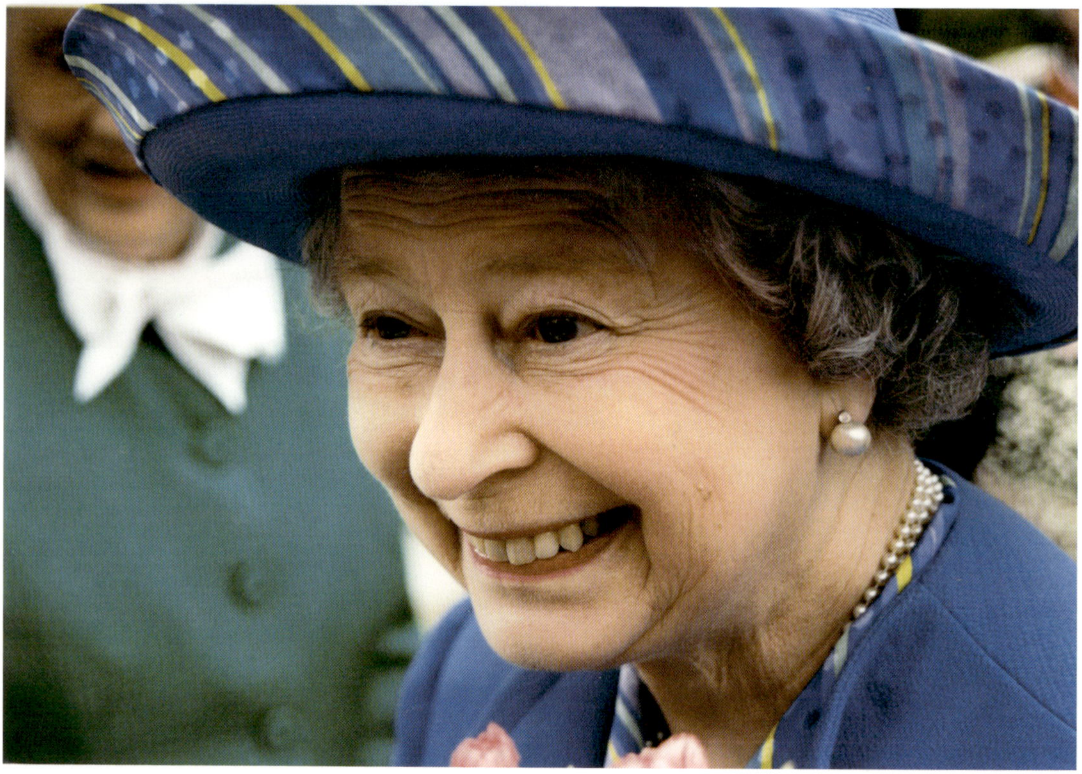

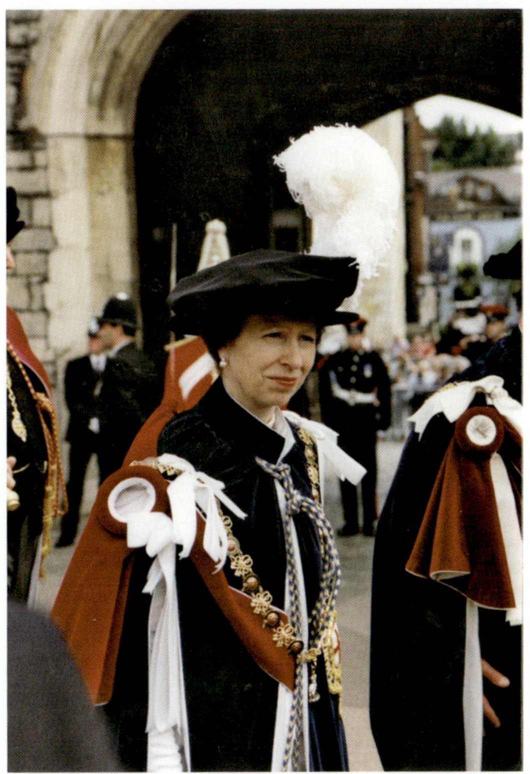

The Garter Ceremony, 14 June 1999
The Princess Royal and Duke of Gloucester were among the members of the Royal Family who attended that year's Order of the Garter Ceremony. The Princess (above) was invested as a Lady Knight five years previously, and always looks happy as she processes to the Chapel.

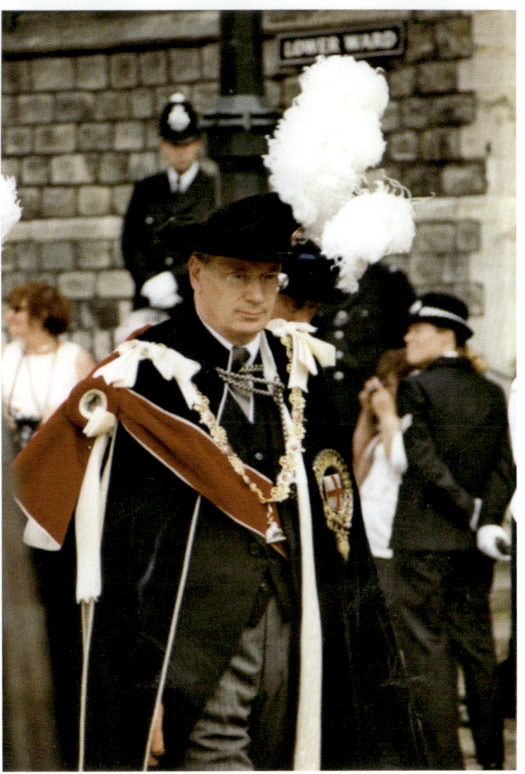

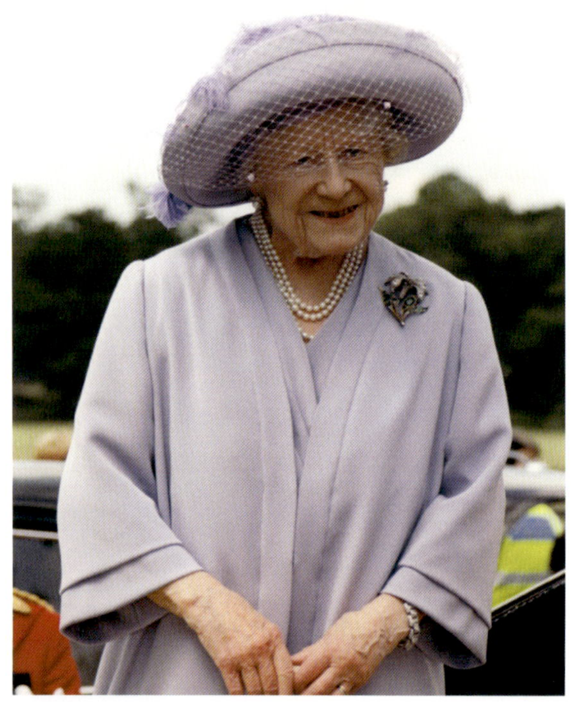

The Queen Mother chose lilac, and the
Queen peach for their outfits for the
summer season highlight of Royal Ascot.
Every day of the Royal meeting, the Royal
party travel by car from Windsor Castle
to the nearby Windsor Great Park, where
at Duke's Lane they transfer from their
cars to the Ascot landau carriages. One
elderly American lady in the crowd passed
a bouquet of spring flowers to the Queen
Mother's carriage, saying 'I'm ninety-nine,
you know' – as quick as a flash the Queen
Mother responded, 'Really ..? You've
beaten me then!'

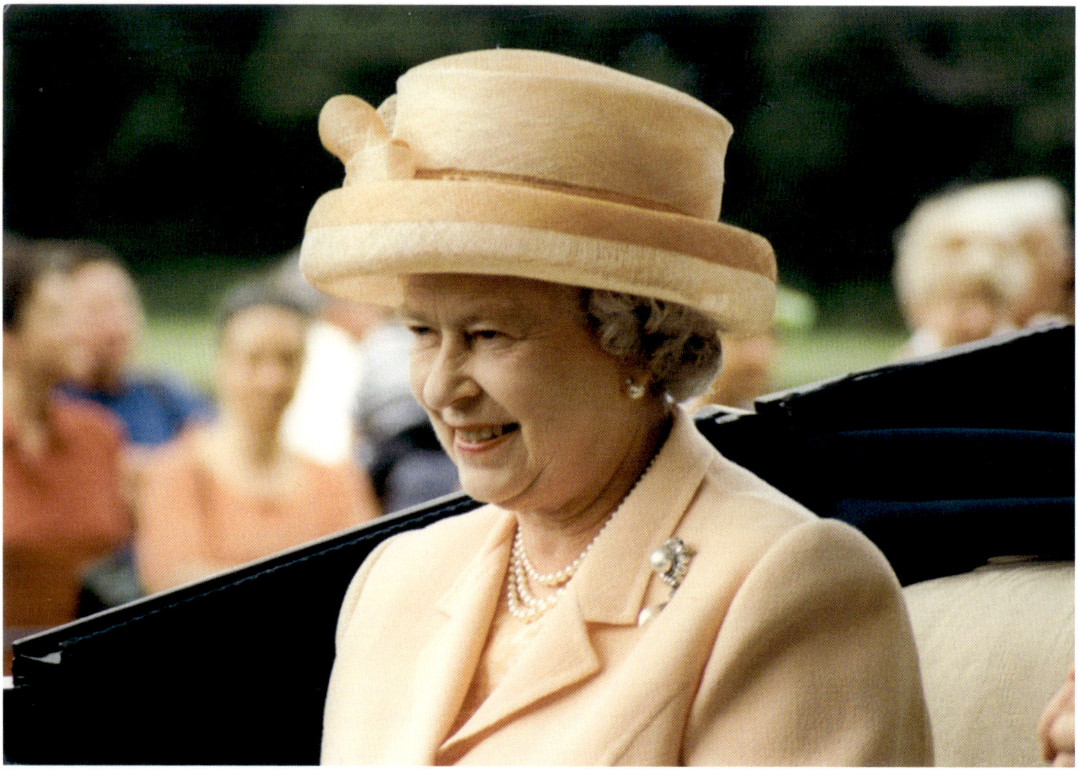

Prince Edward's Wedding, June 1999

The Queen's youngest son married Sophie Rhys Jones in a late afternoon ceremony at Windsor's St George's Chapel. I was fortunate to be the recipient of a ticket allowing me access to the Castle, and had a fantastic view of the Prince and his supporters, Princes Andrew and Charles, walking down from their apartments in the Castle to the Chapel. Afterwards, the newly-married couple returned in an open carriage and into the streets of Windsor to flag-waving crowds.

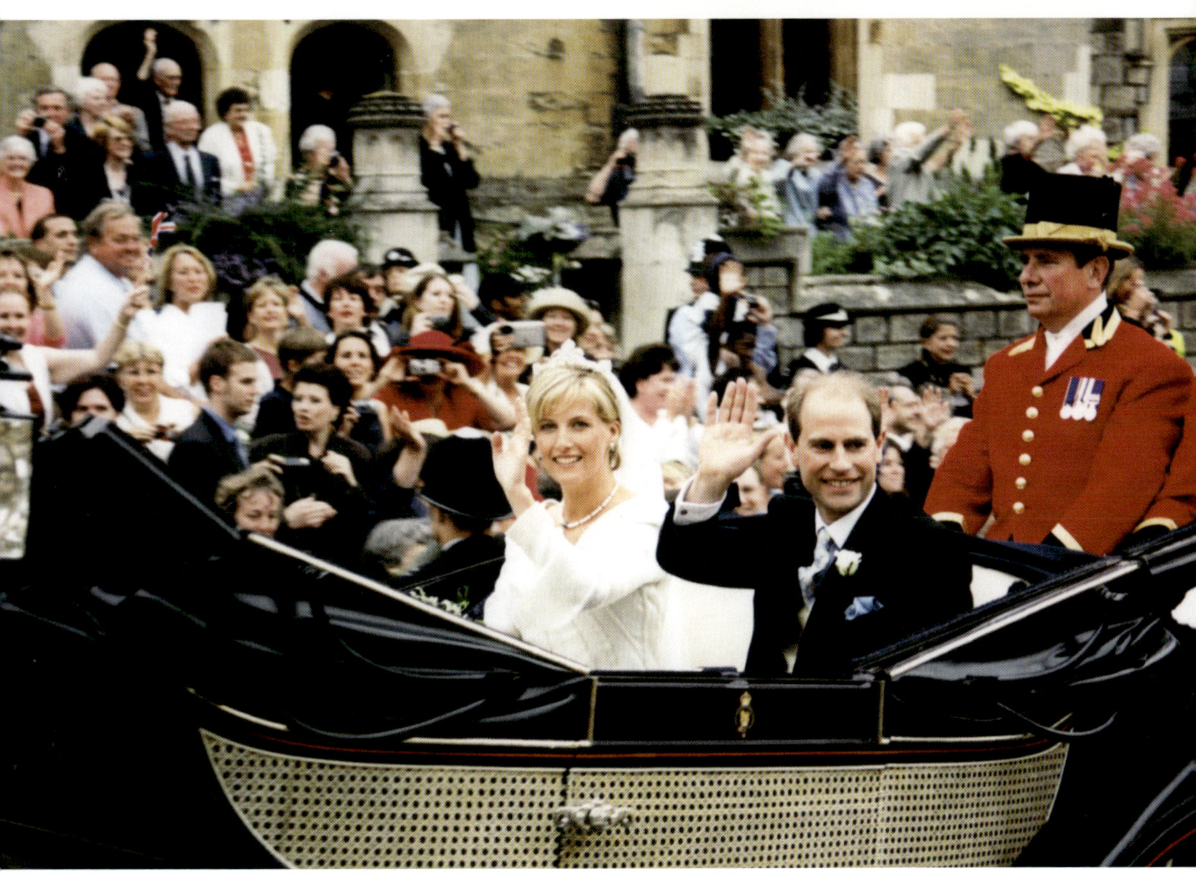

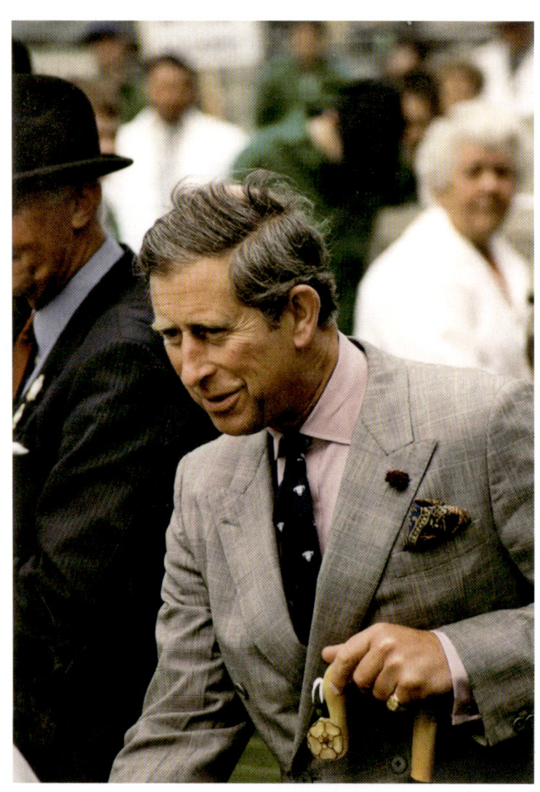

Prince Charles at the Great Yorkshire Show, Harrogate, 15 July 1999

As Patron of the Yorkshire Agricultural Society, Prince Charles attended the last day of the Great Yorkshire Show. The event, held annually over three days in Harrogate, attracts thousands of visitors, and the Prince was given a warm Yorkshire welcome. He used a specially made crook, decorated with the white rose of Yorkshire, to walk around the stands and showground.

Below and opposite:

The Queen and the Duke of Edinburgh, Lancaster and Liverpool, 22 and 23 July 1999

The Queen and her husband started the first day of her two-day northern trip with a visit to the Liverpool Central Library, before attending a reception at the Town Hall.

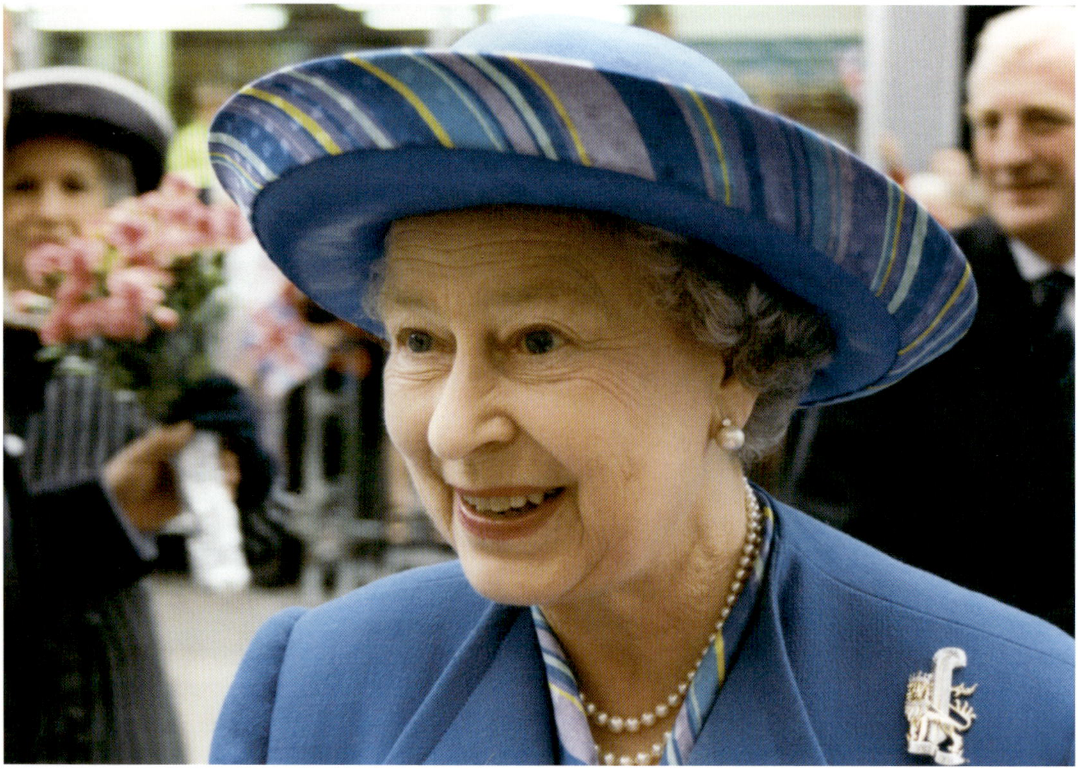

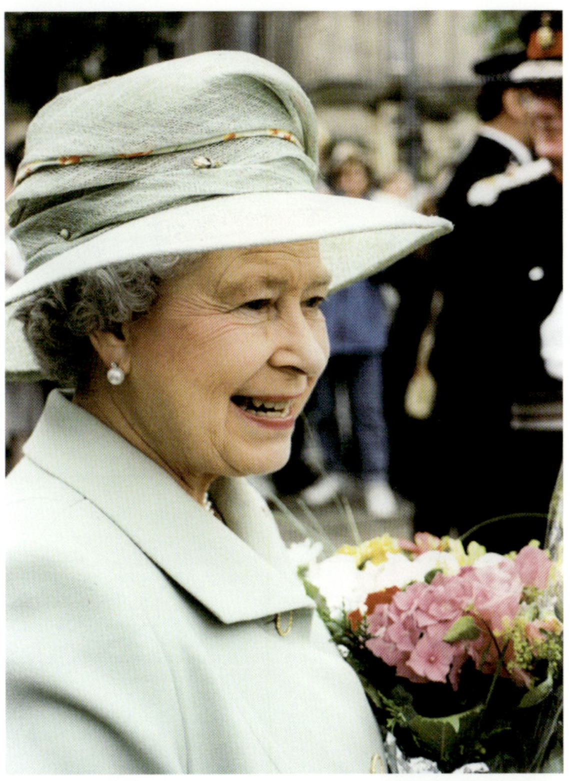

The Queen and the Duke of Edinburgh, Lancaster, 23 July 1999

The Queen holds many titles, the most unusual being the Duchy of Lancaster. So, as the Duke, she visited the market town the next day to mark the 600th anniversary of the link between the Crown and the Duchy (below left). 'Too many hands, too many people to meet,' the Duke joked as he passed well-wishers lined up in the Market Square. On her coat the Queen wore a very special brooch, one with the emblem of the Duchy of Lancaster that she only wears on her visits to the area.

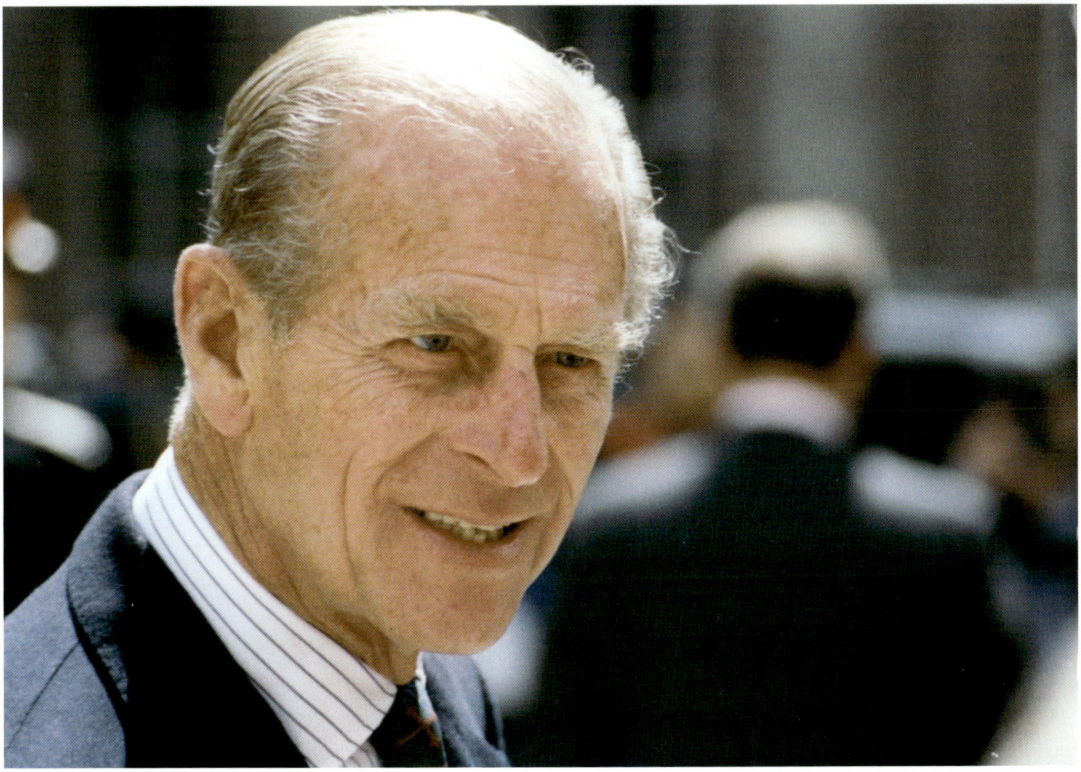

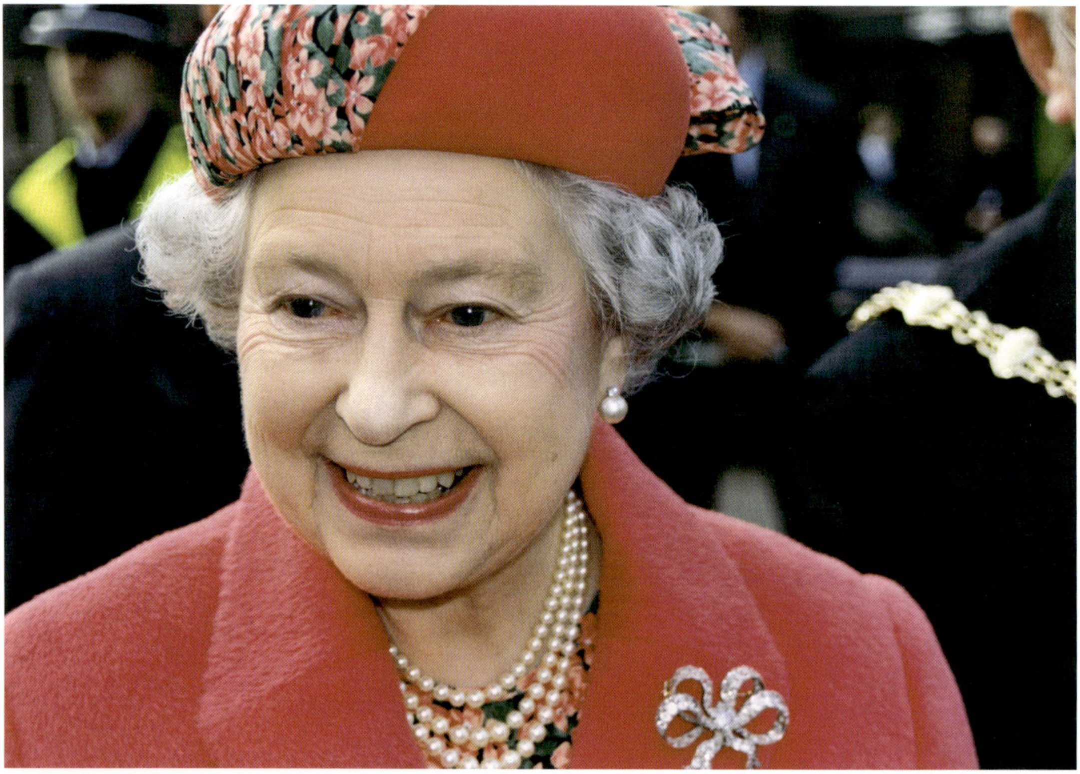

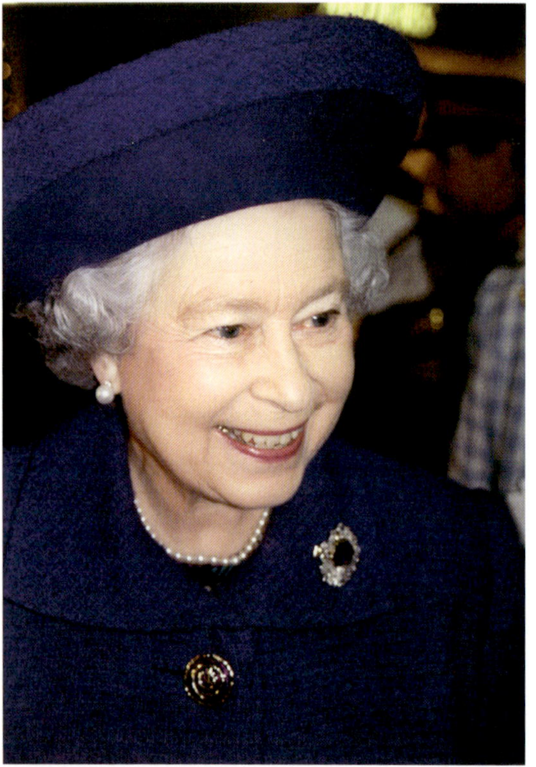

The Queen, Stoke-on-Trent, 28 October 1999
Her first port of call was the city's railway station, where the Royal train arrived, and then it was off for a Royal walkabout in the Potteries area of Hanley town centre.

Left:
The Queen, Nottingham, 9 December 1999
The Queen officially opened the city's new Broadmarsh Shopping Centre, and was smiling broadly as she walked though the precinct, disappearing under armfuls of flowers.

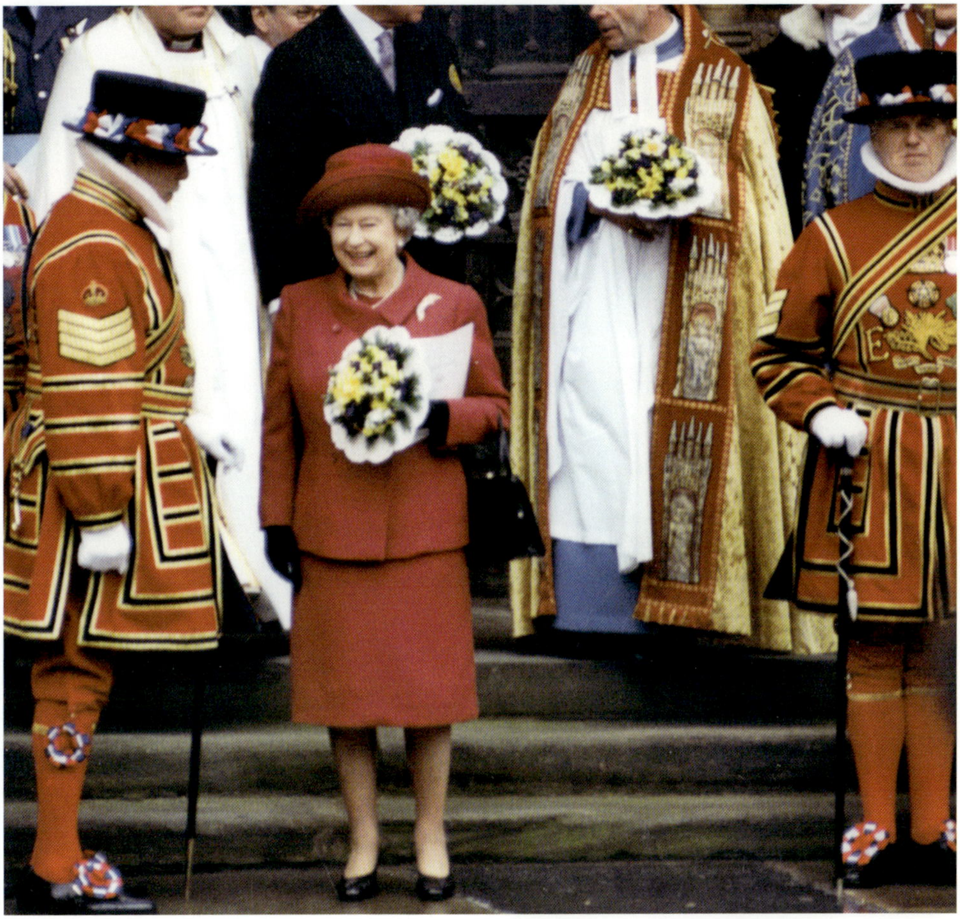

The Queen, Lincoln Cathedral, 20 April 2000

As ever, prior to Easter, the Queen presents
the Royal Maundy, and she visited Lincoln
Cathedral to hand out the Maundy Money to
local pensioners. On the steps of the church she
shared a joke with the Yeoman of the Guard. In
one hand she held the traditional nosegay posy
and the Order of Service as she undertook a
Royal walkabout amongst the large crowds, as
the cathedral bells rang out.

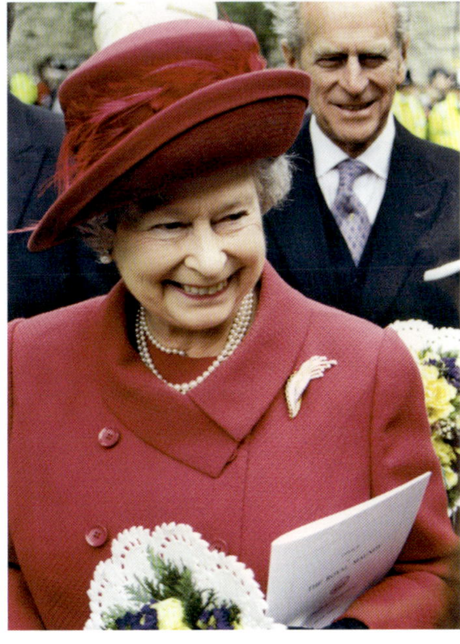

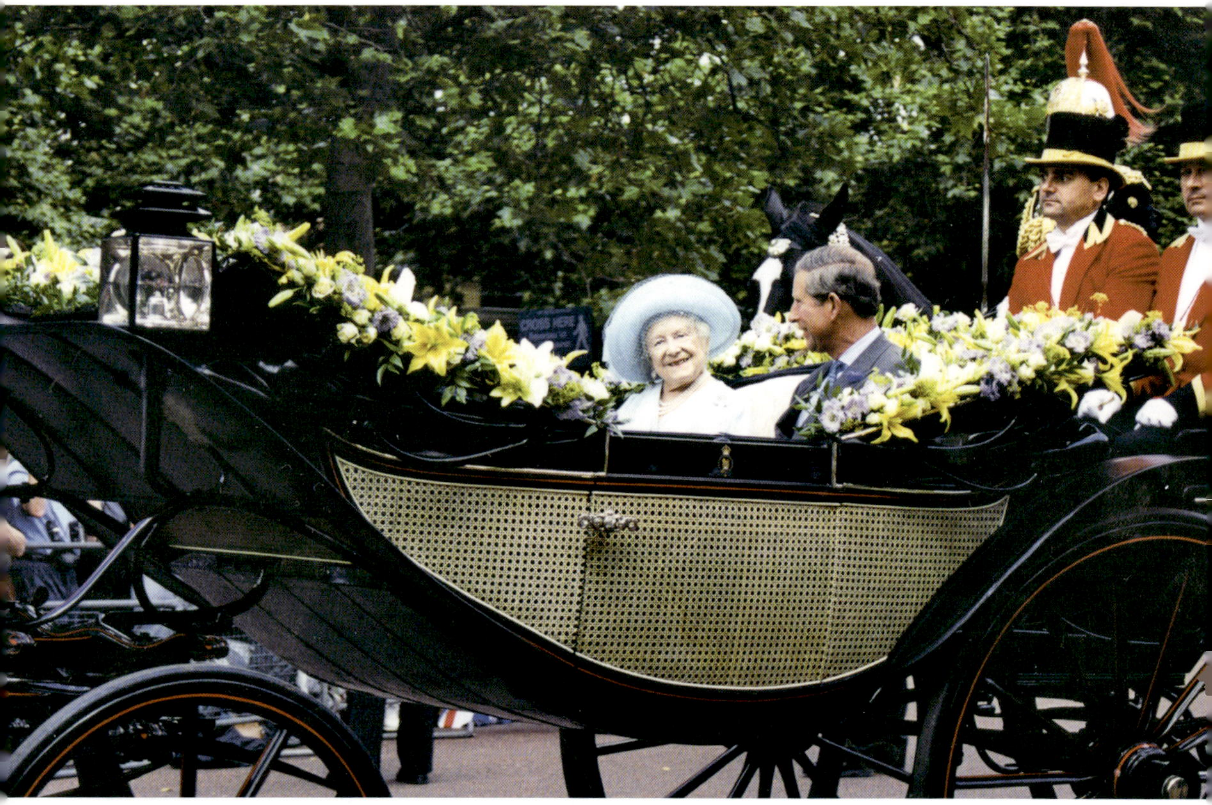

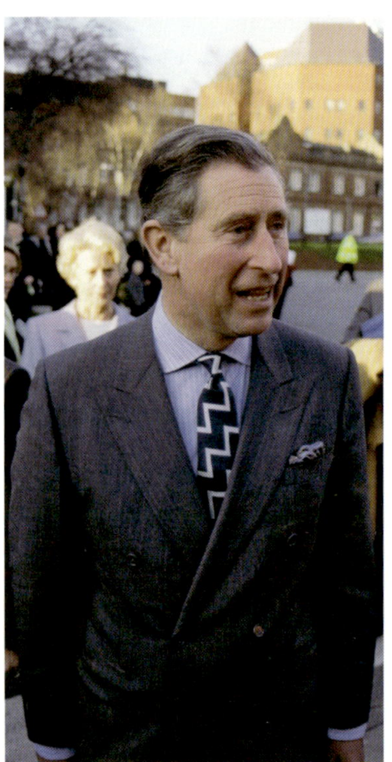

Above:

The Queen Mother's 100th birthday, 4 August 2000

It was a milestone birthday that was celebrated in style. Casting aside the traditions of previous birthday walkabouts, the Queen Mother rode in an open-top carriage procession down The Mall, seated alongside her grandson, Prince Charles, *en route* to Buckingham Palace. The carriage was bedecked in flowers, and she looked genuinely moved by the numbers of people who had come to see her. Earlier in the day she had received, like other centenarians, a birthday telegram form the Queen, although this one was signed not Elizabeth R, but the Queen's pet name of Lilibet.

Left:

Prince Charles, Leeds, 9 February 2001

St James' Hospital in Leeds welcomed Prince Charles when he came to visit the Robert Ogden Macmillan Information Centre. Outside I had the opportunity to present the Prince with a photograph from his grandmother's 100th birthday. 'Didn't it all look so lovely, the carriage with the flowers? She is much better and is getting back to her old self now.' He also joked how the Queen Mother was so little; 'all you probably saw was a hat as she passed by.'

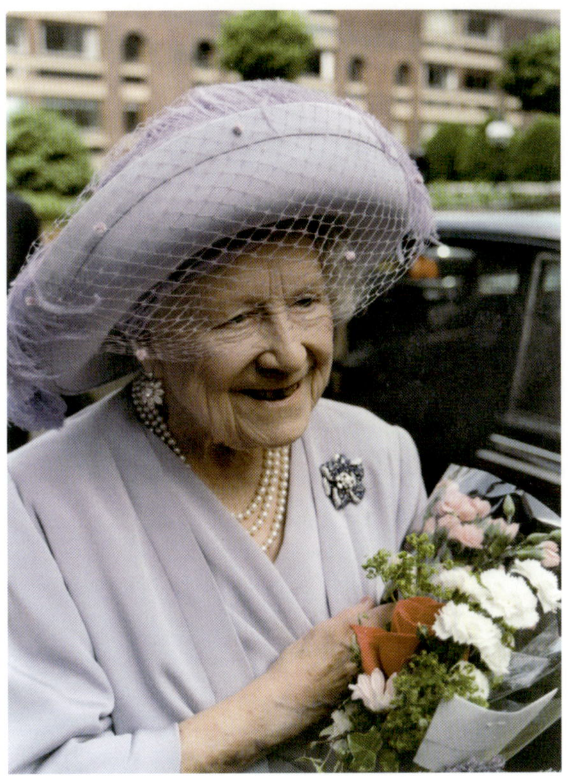

Right:
**The Queen Mother, London,
27 June 2001**
After many health scares, the Queen
Mother continued her workload at the
age of nearly 101. Here she visited the
Worshipful Company of Barber Surgeons'
Hall, to lunch with the Master and Court
of Assistants.

Below:
**Prince Charles, Bradford,
3 September 2001**
Visiting the new £5.2 million Marie Curie
Hospice in Bradford, Prince Charles
accepted a beautiful white rose buttonhole
from an admirer in the crowd, who with
his consent pinned in onto his lapel.

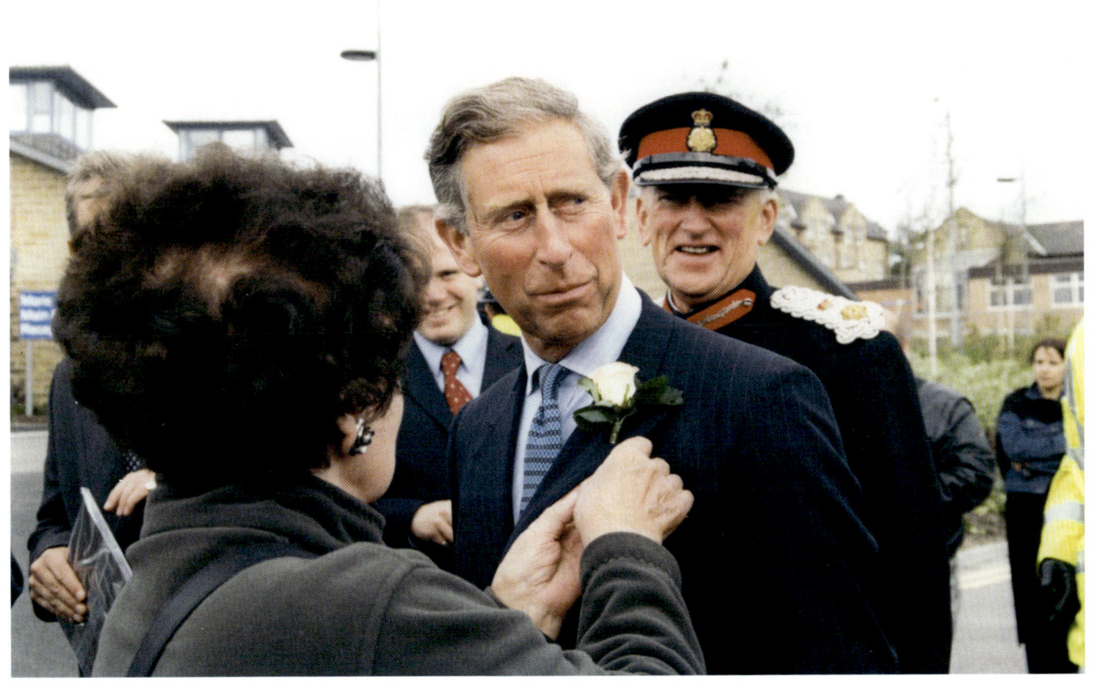

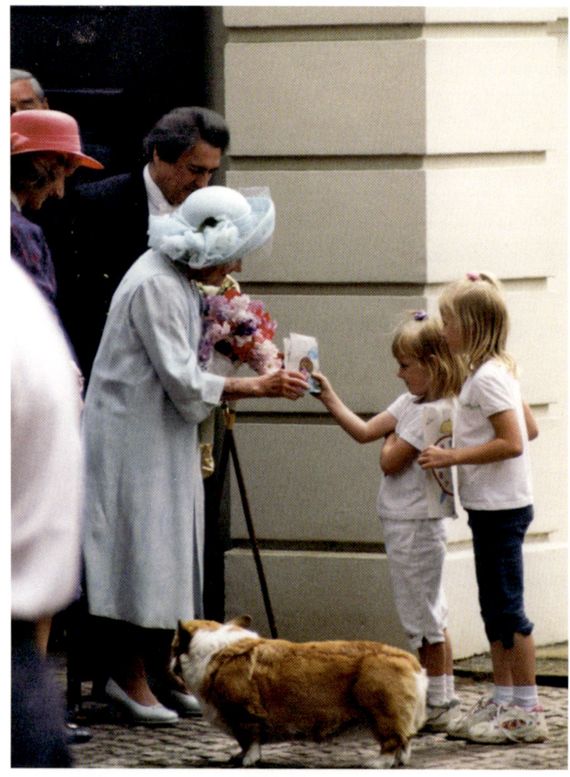

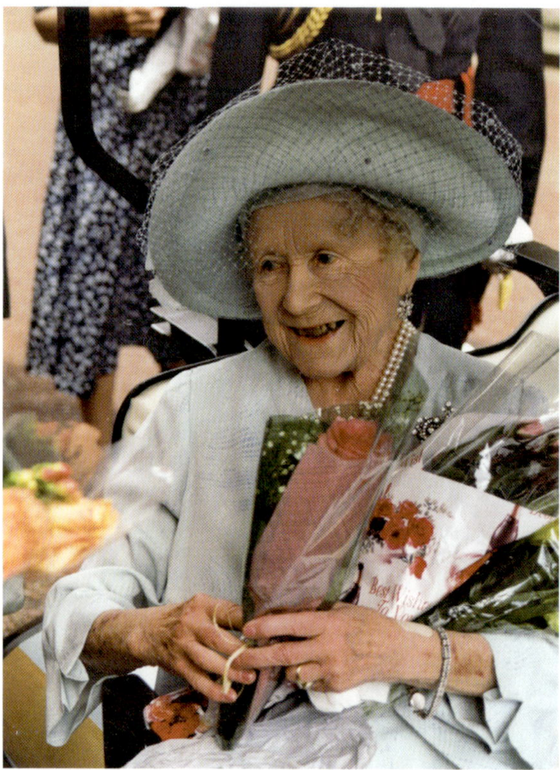

The Queen Mother's 101st Birthday, 4 August 2001

Her appearance on her birthday had been the cause of much speculation as her frailty became more apparent. However, never one to disappoint her public, and despite the obvious efforts it took, the Queen Mother appeared at the gates of Clarence House and stood for a long time whilst children all lined up to present her with their flowers, gifts and cards. Even the Royal corgis came out to have a nosey! Then it was into the Royal Buggy to be driven around the crowds, before she was joined by her extended family for one final wave before lunch beneath the trees in the Clarence House gardens.

Right:

The Queen Mother's 101st Birthday, 4 August 2001

The Queen Mother, pictured in her golf buggy, wears a special brooch on her chiffon dress. The Jubilee Brooch was originally given to Queen Victoria by her Royal Household in 1897 to mark the Diamond Jubilee.

Below:

Celebrations at Clarence House

Accompanying the Queen Mother as she appears at the famous gates of Clarence House are: Princess Beatrice (head turned from the camera), Peter Phillips, Princess Anne and her husband Tim, the Queen, Princess Eugenie and the Duke of York.

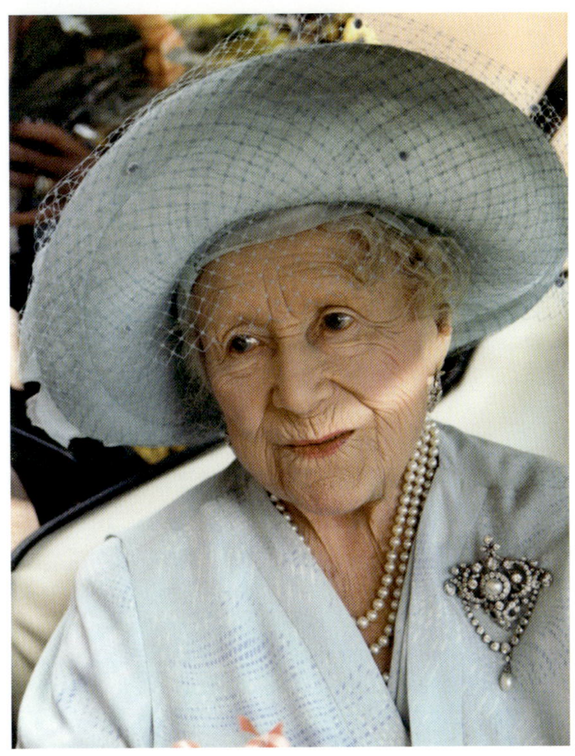

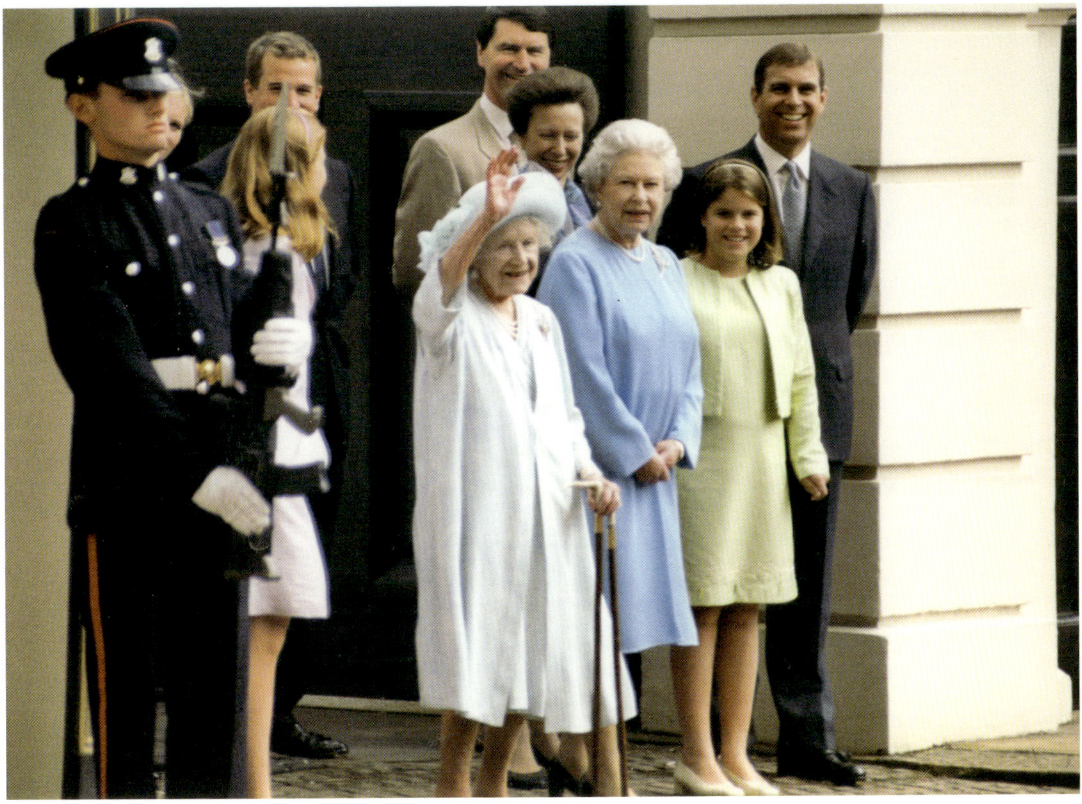

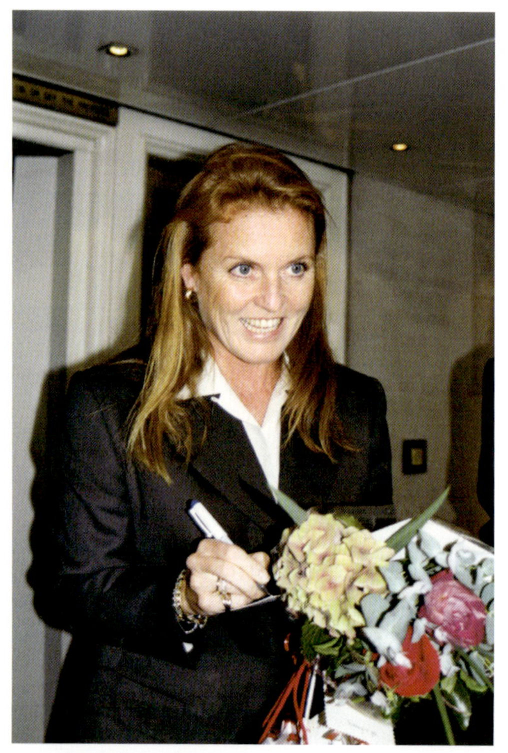

Memories of 9/11 were still fresh in everyone's minds when the Duchess of York arrived at the Queen's Hotel in Leeds to attend a charity dinner there in aid of her charity, Children in Crisis. As she arrived she handed out cards for 'The Duchess of York's 9/11 Fund', in memory of those who lost their lives in the twin-tower attacks in the USA, autographing some as a keepsake. Her American charity had offices in the World Trade Centre, and the Duchess herself was in New York at the time of the attacks. When she arrived, a *Big Issue* vendor approached her and she duly bought a copy, with an aide handing over £5. A cause for some hilarity – a young girl working for a nightclub (dressed as a playing card!), tried to hand over a flyer to her. 'Does your mother know you dress like that?' she joked.

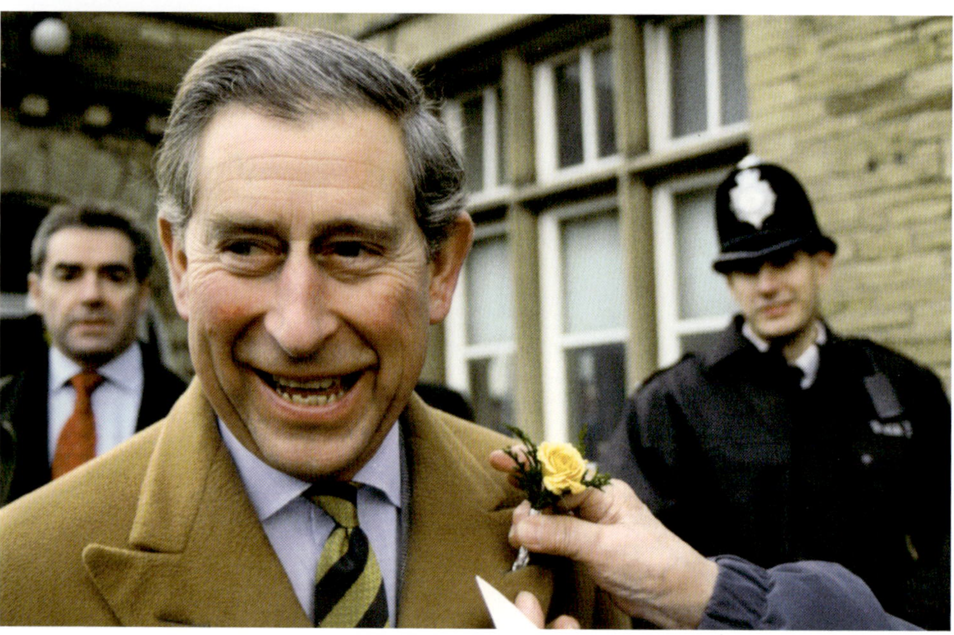

Prince Charles, Skipton, 17 December 2001
With the country getting over the worst case of Foot and Mouth to hit the farming community for some time, Prince Charles paid a morale-boosting visit to North Yorkshire. He was cheered by onlookers as he arrived, snugly dressed in a three-quarter-length camel overcoat, at Skipton's railway station.

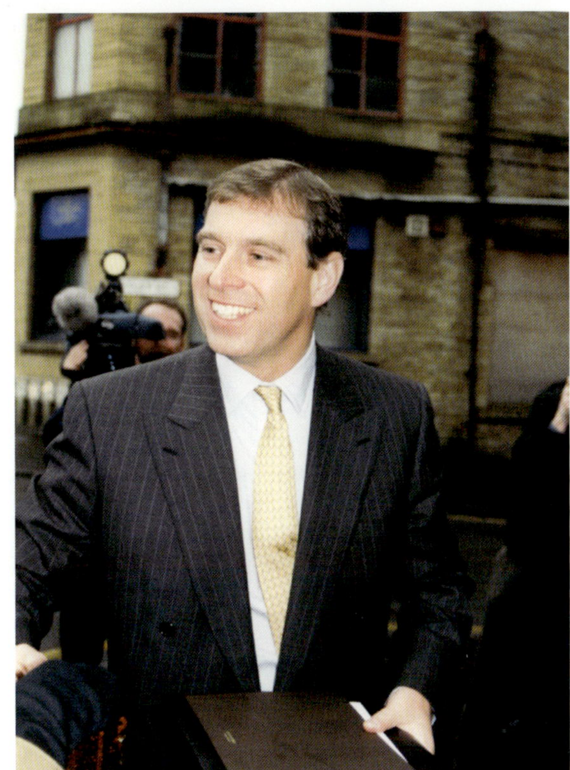

**Prince Andrew, Bradford,
18 December 2001**
Presenting one of his Duke of York
Community Initiative Awards, Prince
Andrew arrived at the Woolston House
Business Centre in Bradford, where he
attended a reception.

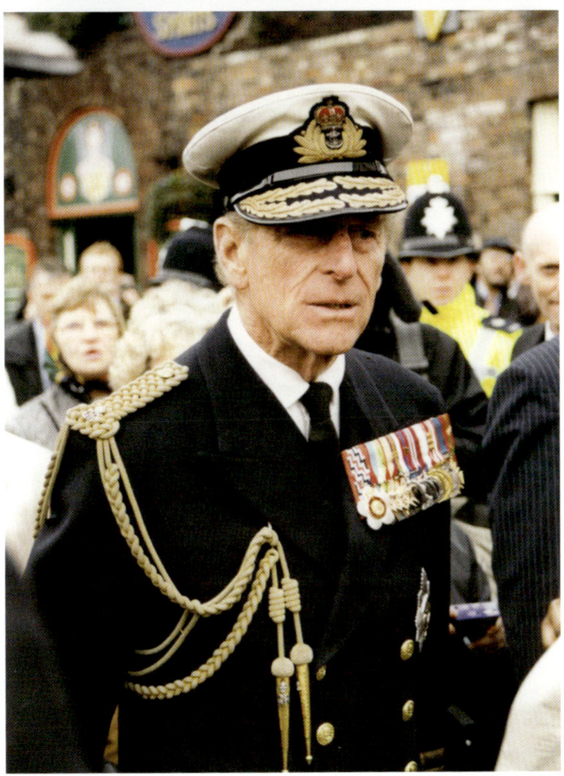

**The Duke of Edinburgh, King's Lynn,
4 February 2002**
After attending morning service with the
Queen, the Duke of Edinburgh, dressed
in uniform, arrived in Kings Lynn to take
the salute at a march past to mark the
eightieth anniversary of the Kings Lynn
branch of the Royal British Legion. HRH
is a life member of the branch.

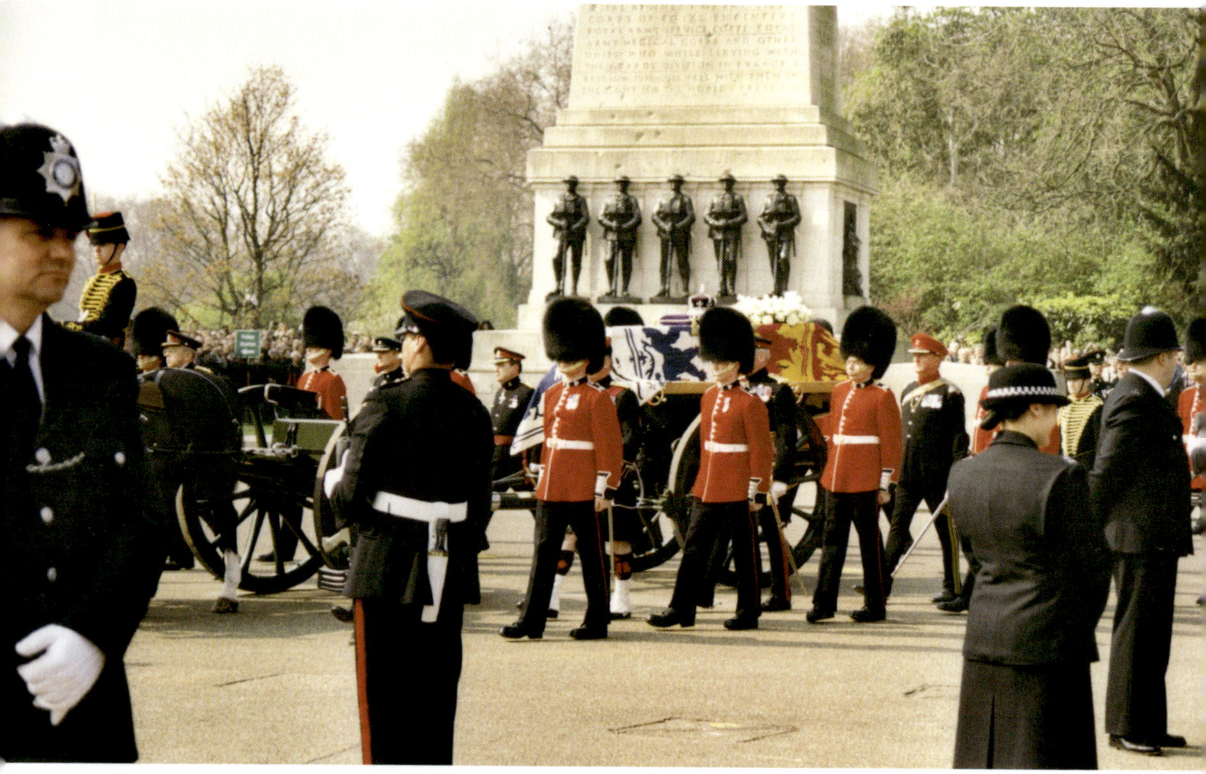

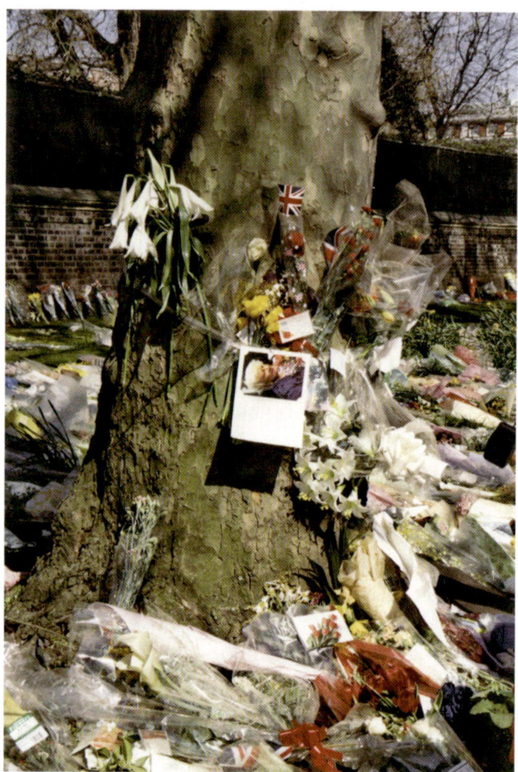

The Queen Mother's Funeral Cortège, London, 5 April 2002

When she died on 31 March 2002, the Queen Mother left a huge void in the hearts of so many. As the cortège carrying her coffin on top of a gun carriage wound its way through Horse Guards Parade, it was indeed a moving sight to witness. On top of her coffin was the crown she had worn at her Coronation in 1937. For the Queen, her mother's death came only weeks after that of her sister, Princess Margaret. The sun shone that April day as she was carried to lie in state at Westminster Hall, prior to her funeral service at Westminster Abbey. I was one of the thousands who queued for hours to pay my respects, and that day in Westminster Hall, with the Yeomen of the Guard standing vigil, was one of the most memorable things I have witnessed.

Left:
Floral tributes outside Clarence House, London. A poignant reminder of the very great affection felt for the Quuen Mother.

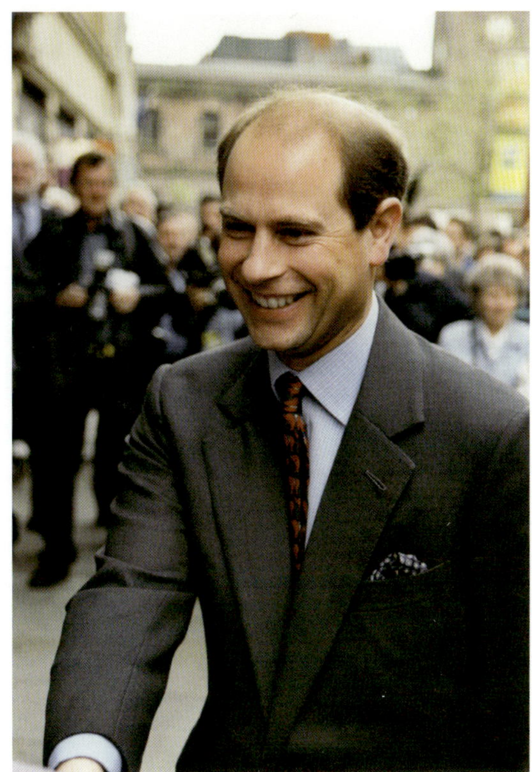

Prince Edward and Countess Sophie, Manchester, 22 April 2002
As Patron of the Royal Exchange Theatre in Manchester, Prince Edward, and his wife Sophie, arrived to attend a fund-raising lunch. 'You'll be seeing a lot more of us', the Countess said.

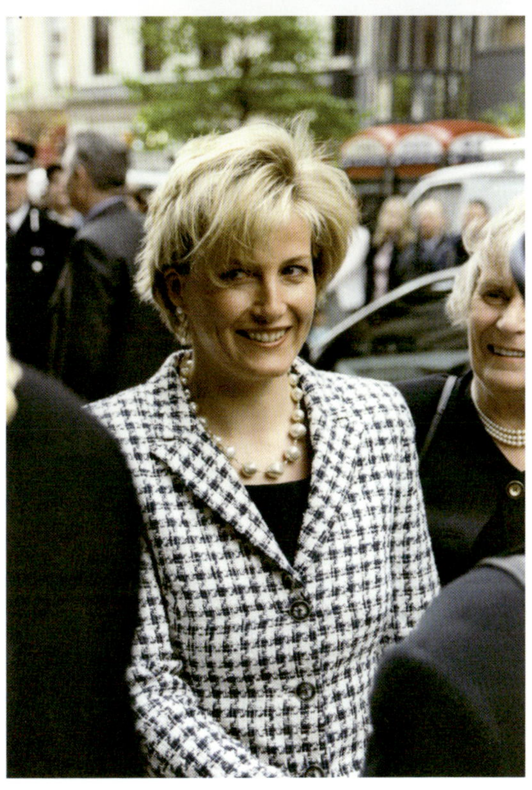

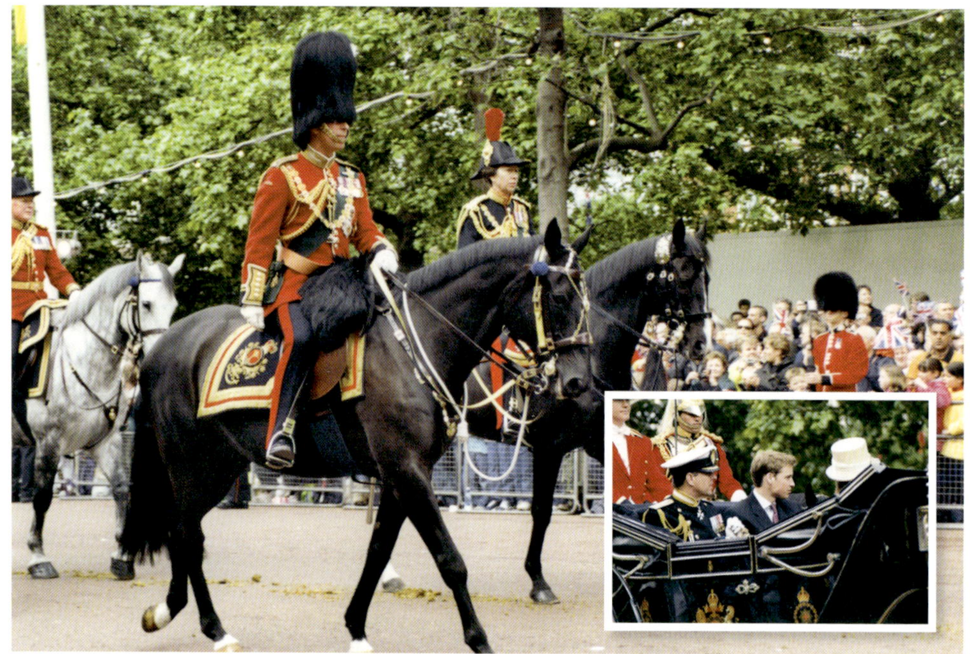

Golden Jubilee Day, London, June 2002

Fifty years ago, a young Princess became Queen Elizabeth II, and today, with her family beside her, the main Golden Jubilee events started with a historic procession down The Mall in the gold State Coach. With Prince Charles and Princess Anne riding behind her on horseback, they made their way to a service of thanksgiving at St Paul's Cathedral. Other members of the family rode in carriages, with Prince William sitting next to his uncle, Prince Andrew.

The day was given a party atmosphere. The night before there had been the Party at the Palace concert, and on this day the Notting Hill Carnival was to take centre stage. Leading the Queen down, in the ceremonial Land Rover, were throngs of schoolchildren waving golden streamers. Both she and Prince Philip stood up to acknowledge the enormous support that the public gave them as they came into sight, The Queen even directed her chauffeur to drive more centrally by frantically waving her arms! With Concorde flying overhead, and 'Land of Hope and Glory' echoing around, it was indeed a great weekend.

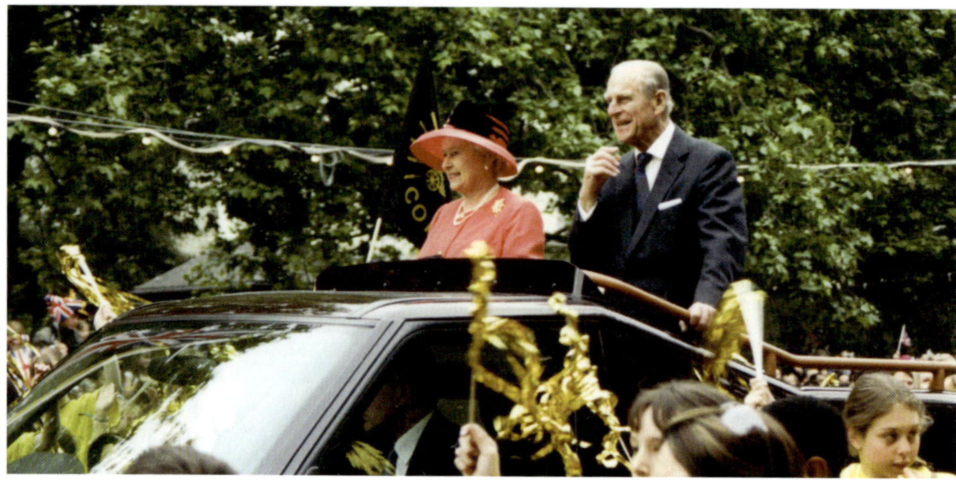

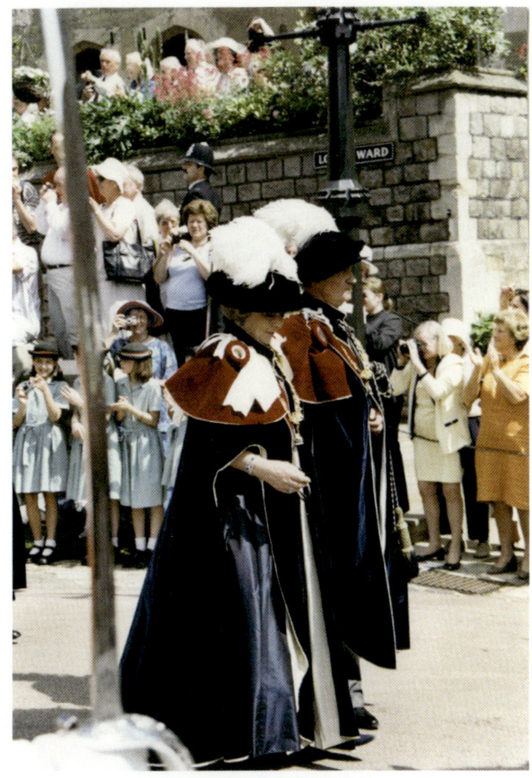

The Garter Ceremony, June 2002

To mark the Golden Jubilee, this year's Order of the Garter held a special significance, as heads of state from many European countries, all of whom hold the highest personal honour the Queen bestows, attended the pageantry, including King Harald V of Norway (attending the ceremony to be invested as a Knight), King Juan Carlos of Spain, Queen Beatrix of the Netherlands (above right), Queen Margrethe of Denmark and Grand Duke Jean of Luxembourg (below right). The Garter started when it was rumoured in the fourteenth century, King Edward III picked up the garter of Joan, Countess of Salisbury. Rather than chastise her, the King said '*Honi soit qui mal y pense*' ('Evil to him who Evil thinks'); that remark remains the motto of the Order to this day.

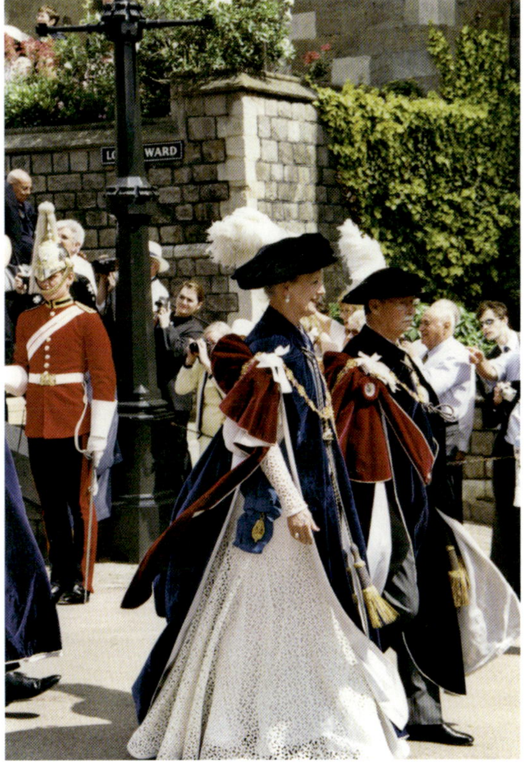

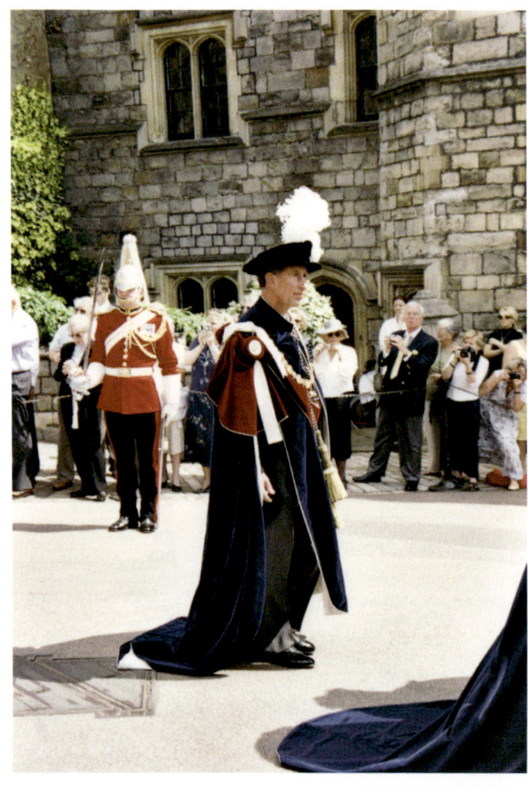

Prince Charles at the Garter Ceremony, June 2002
Many members of the public can be seen in the background taking photographs and enjoying the ceremony.

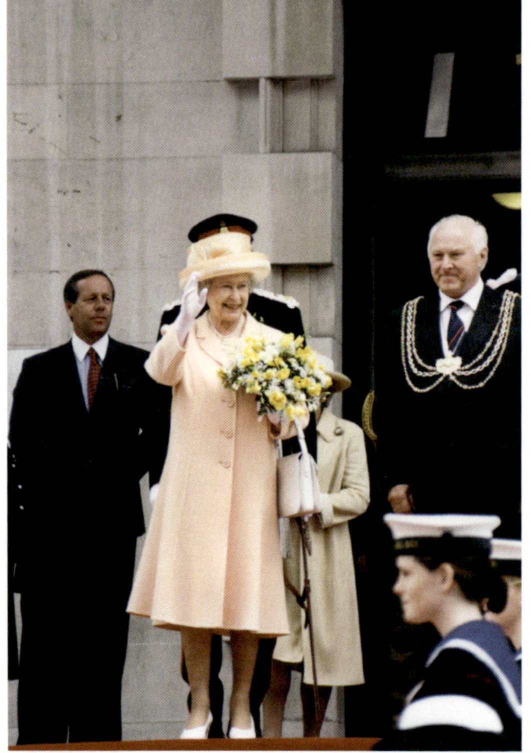

Her Majesty The Queen, Leeds, 11 July 2002
With the Golden Jubilee tour of the country well underway, it was the start of the northern leg of her visit when the Queen arrived in Leeds. As she made her way down the red carpet on the steps of the Civic Hall, there was an honour guard made up of Sea Cadets. It had been a busy day for the monarch, with a visit to the set of the soap opera *Emmerdale*, and a garden party at Harewood House, the home of her cousin, the Earl of Harewood.

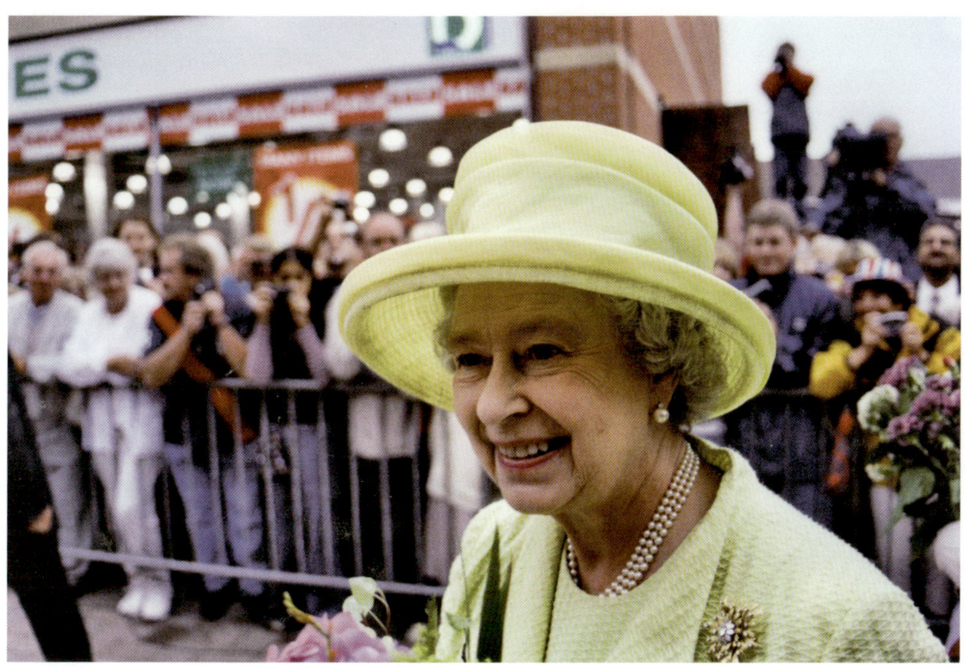

Her Majesty The Queen and the Duke of Edinburgh, Scunthorpe, 31 July 2002
The town of Scunthorpe paid host to the Queen and her husband. They arrived on the Royal train (their temporary home as they travelled the length and breadth of the country), with the Jubilee tour of the UK drawing to an end. While the Prince visited an arts centre, the Queen walked through the town centre, escorted by the mayor.

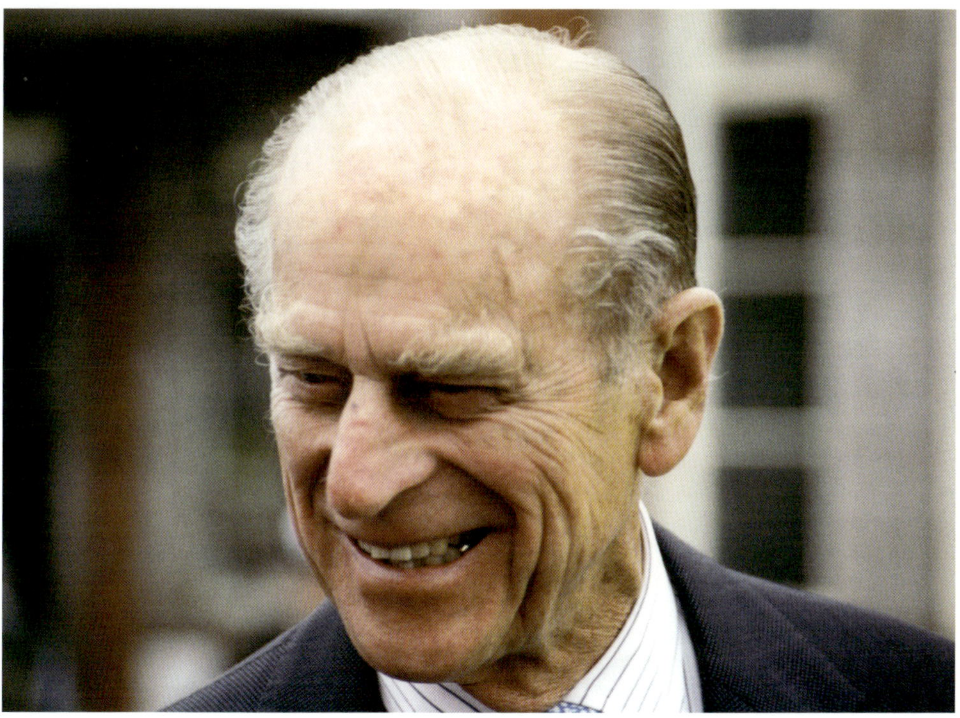

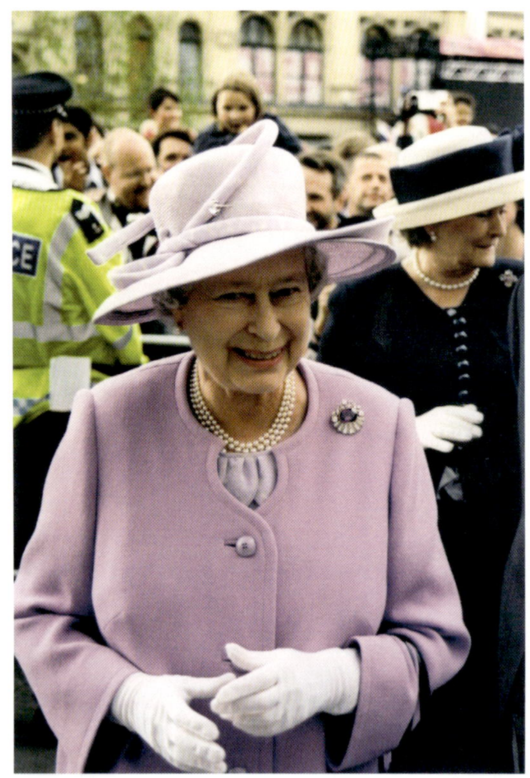

Her Majesty The Queen, Manchester, 24 July 2002
When a bomb destroyed some of the city centre of Manchester, the determination to re-build was at the forefront of most people's minds, and here the Queen visited Manchester to see for herself how the regeneration had changed the area. She walked through Exchange Square, meeting the crowds. The city was already on a high with the Commonwealth Games (which she opened the following night), and to have the Queen visit was indeed the icing on the cake. She later attended a service of thanksgiving for the restoration of the city centre at the cathedral.

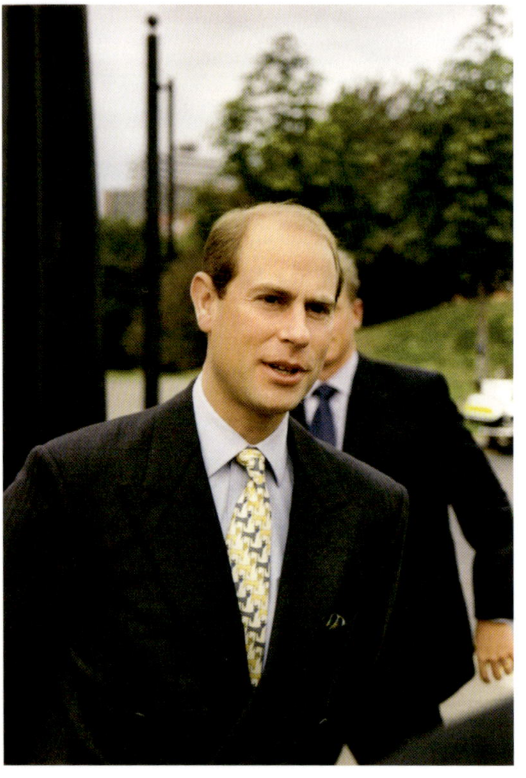

Prince Edward, Leeds, September 2002
Visiting with the Countess, Prince Edward visited the West Yorkshire Playhouse to spearhead a £9 million campaign to open the headquarters for the Northern Ballet Theatre. They attended the press launch for the campaign, before that night attending a performance of the ballet's production of *Wuthering Heights* at the Alhambra Theatre in Bradford.

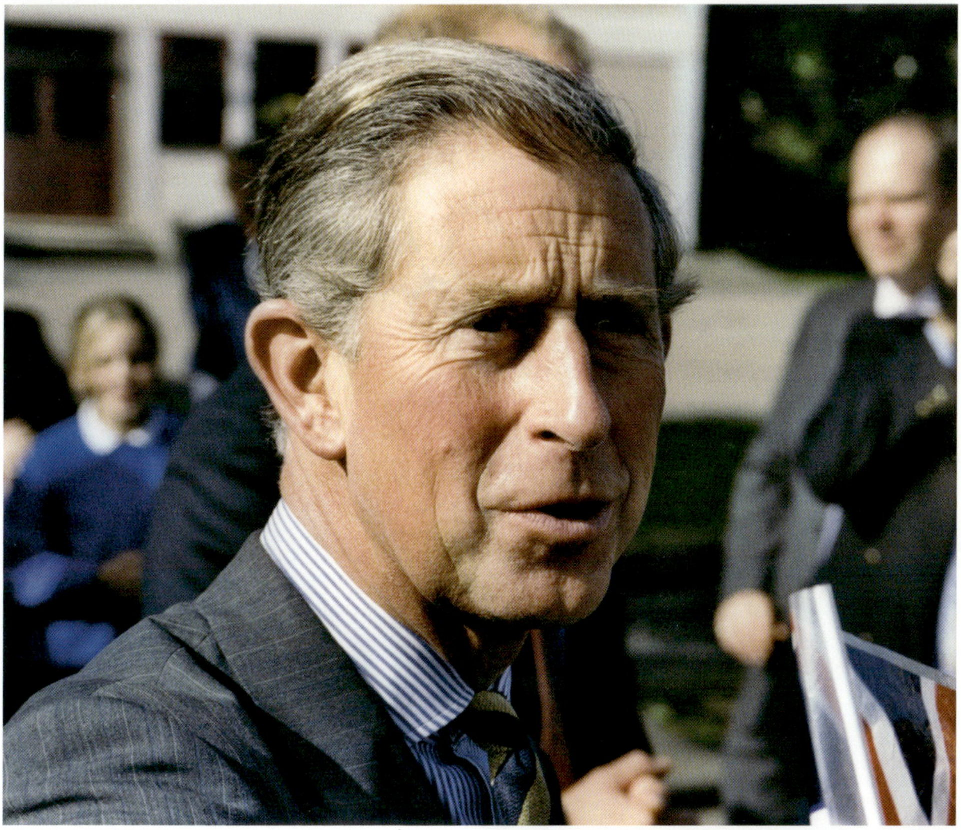

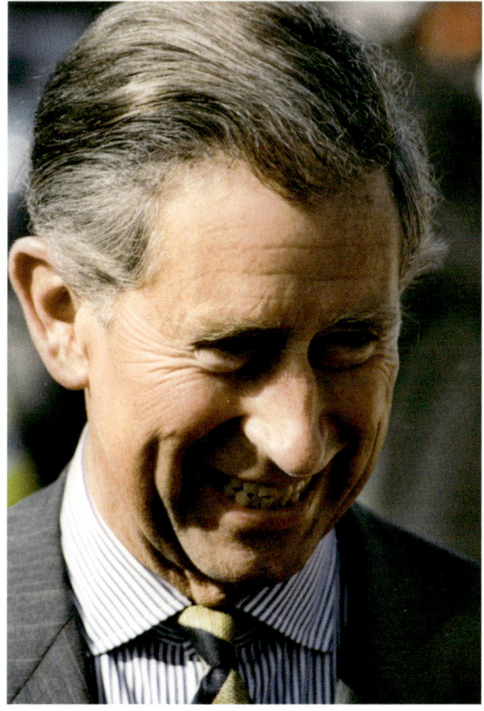

Prince Charles, Bradford,
30 September 2002

Prince Charles came to Bradford to attend the rededication of the war memorial in Cottingley, Bradford. The memorial had been vandalised, and the day was to unify the community. He was led into the parish church of St Michael and All Angels for a short service before the rededication ceremony. He then embarked on a thirty-minute walkabout and met literally hundreds of locals, all desperate to shake his hand. 'Will you be going into the pub?' he enquired. 'I've just met the pub owner – what a nice man', he added.

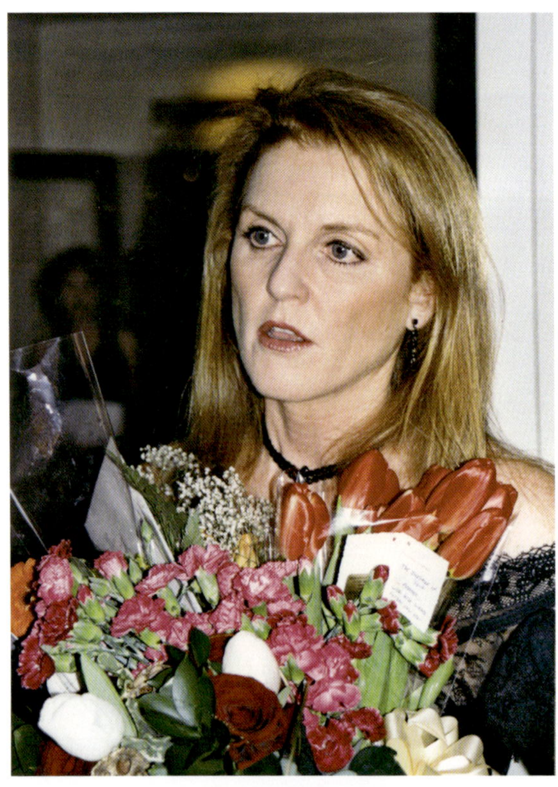

**The Duchess of York, Leeds,
10 December 2002**
The Duchess of York was the guest of honour at a dinner at Leeds' Queen's Hotel for her charity Children in Crisis, and the Duchess looked stunning in a black lace gown as she accepted flowers.

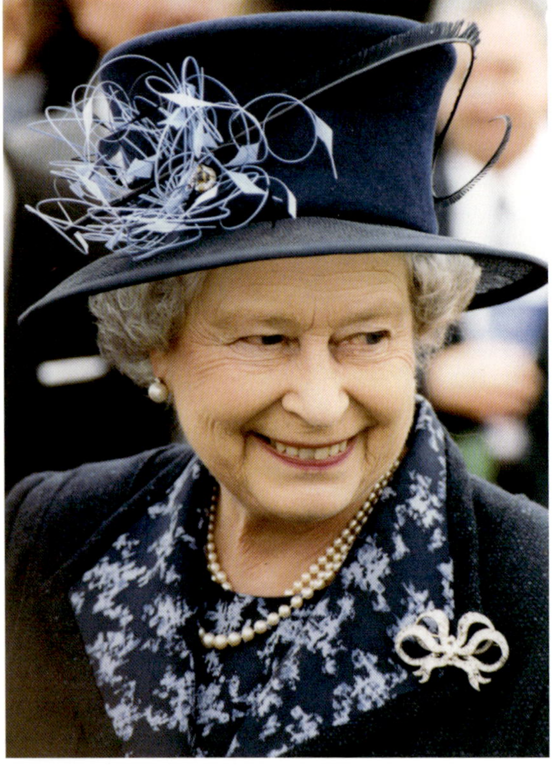

**Her Majesty The Queen, Wrexham,
4 June 2003**
The Queen visited Wrexham College to see the 'TechniQuest' event – an opportunity to see at first hand the science discovery centre, and be interactive! A series of inter-linked marquees showed how Wrexham had re-generated, and also gave the Queen an insight into the world of science.

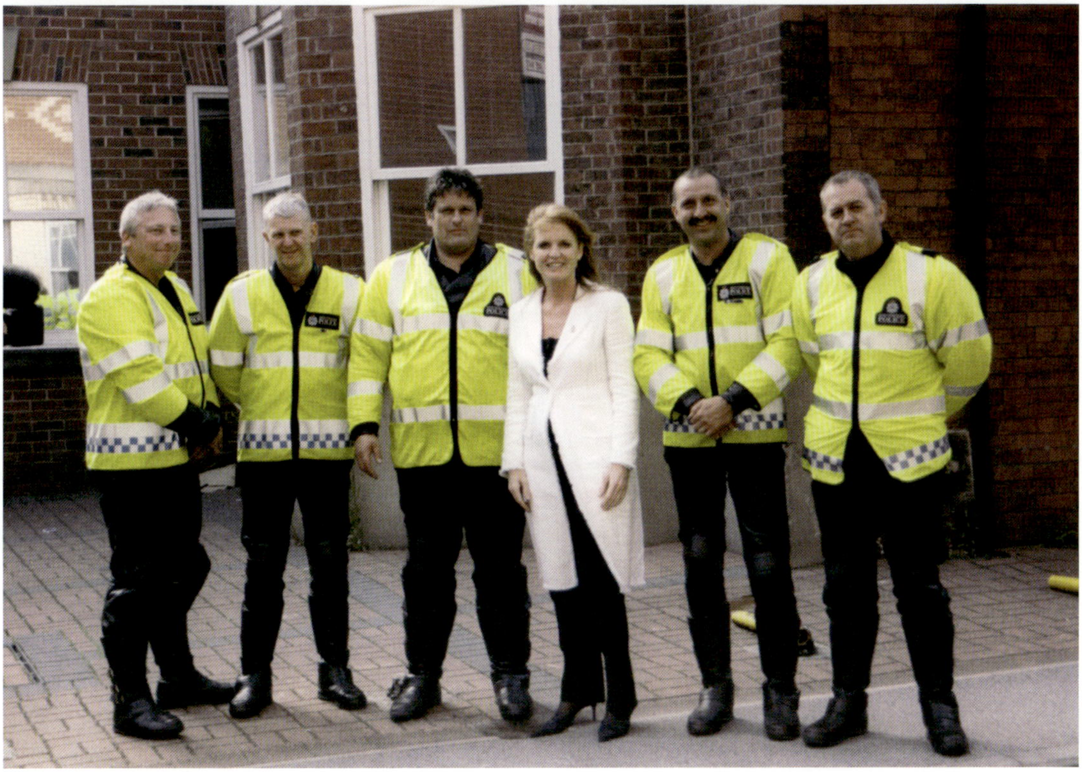

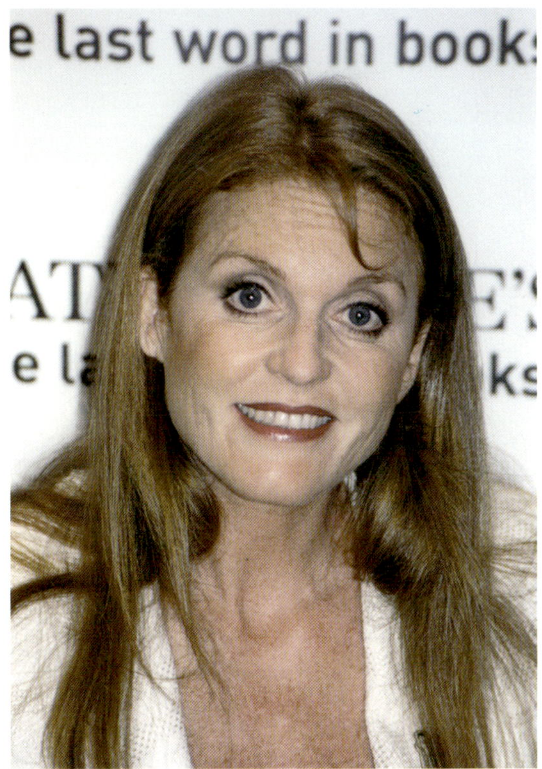

The Duchess of York, Leeds, 25 June 2003
Visiting a Leeds bookshop, Sarah Duchess of York was doing a book-signing to promote her book *Moments*. There was the unusual sight of seeing her arrive with a police motorbike escort. To say thank you she decided to have her photograph taken and asked me to take it! 'Paul, can you send copies to them?' she said, gesturing to the policemen. "Well, I'll send them to you, and then you can do the necessary.' Giving a thumbs-up, she added, 'Fantastic – I'll sign them too!'

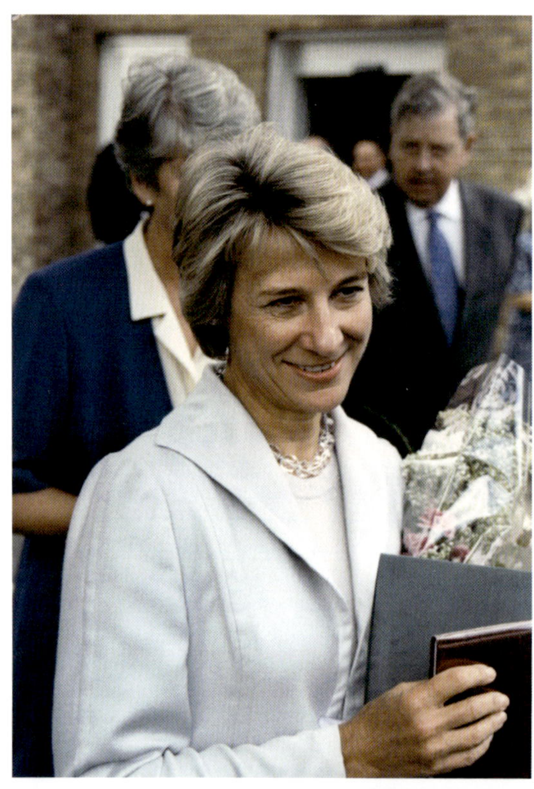

**The Duchess of Gloucester, Sheffield,
3 September 2003**
St Luke's Hospice in Sheffield welcomed
the Duchess of Gloucester as she came to
open their new patients' lift. The Duchess
charmed the patients with her relaxed
approach, and before she left had a look
round the Hospice gardens.

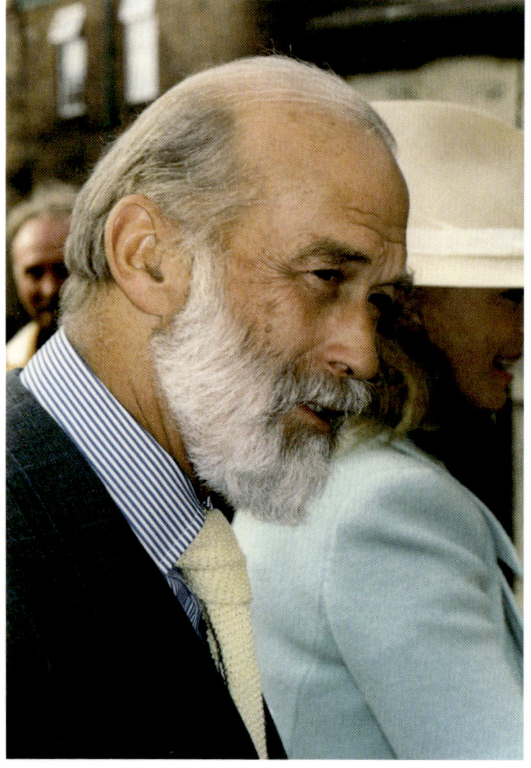

**Prince Michael of Kent, Howden,
7 September 2003**
Prince Michael had just attended the third
annual Howden Festival with his wife,
Princess Michael. The following day the Royal
couple attended a service at Howden Minster,
where the choir of HM Chapel Royal sang.
On their arrival at the festival, I had given
Princess Michael a photograph of the last
time I had seen her several years ago. 'Oh,
that must be quite recent', she enquired. 'Well
actually Ma'am', I replied, 'it's eight years ago.'
Pulling a face she said, 'Oh no! It can't be! In
fact I'm going to wear that outfit tomorrow
– don't tell anyone – it's a secret!'

The Royal couple had a packed day of engagements for their Derbyshire tour. In the morning the Queen attended a service at Derby Cathedral, before opening the new Derby Cathedral Centre. In the afternoon they met up to tour Chesterfield, but the change in weather called for a change in costume as the Royal raincoats were used! Touring Chesterfield's Open Market, the Queen and Duke, umbrellas in hand, walked around greeting stallholders. One chap in the crowd even tried to stir naval memories for the Duke by remembering a ship they both served on!

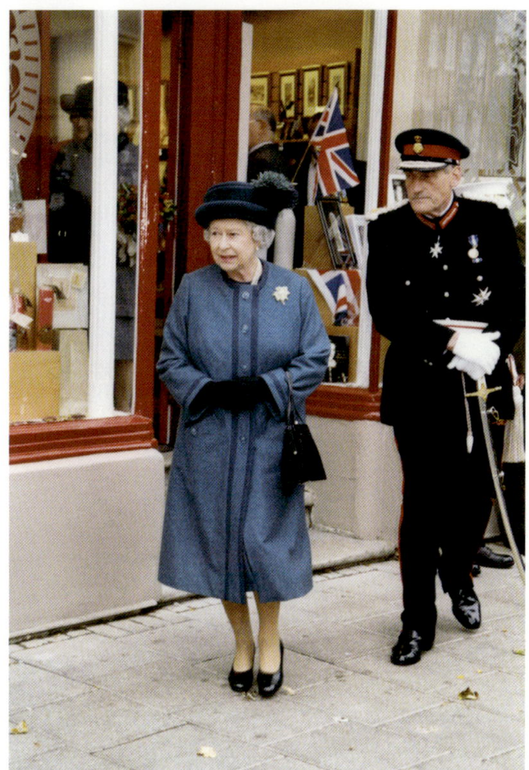

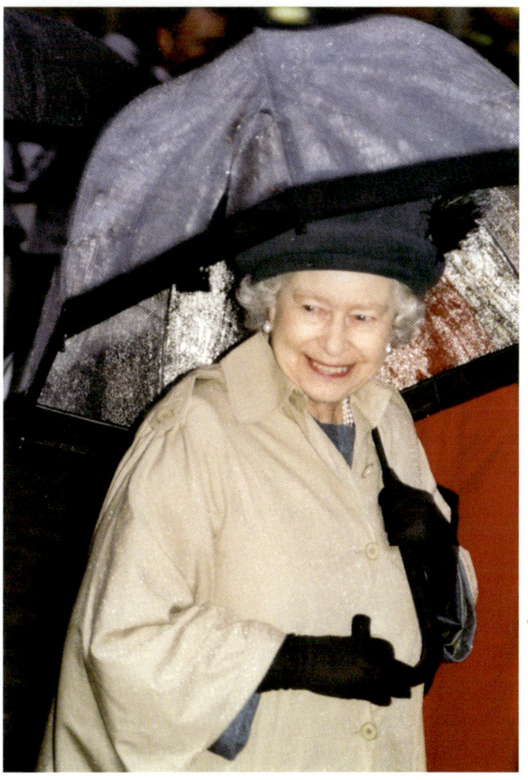

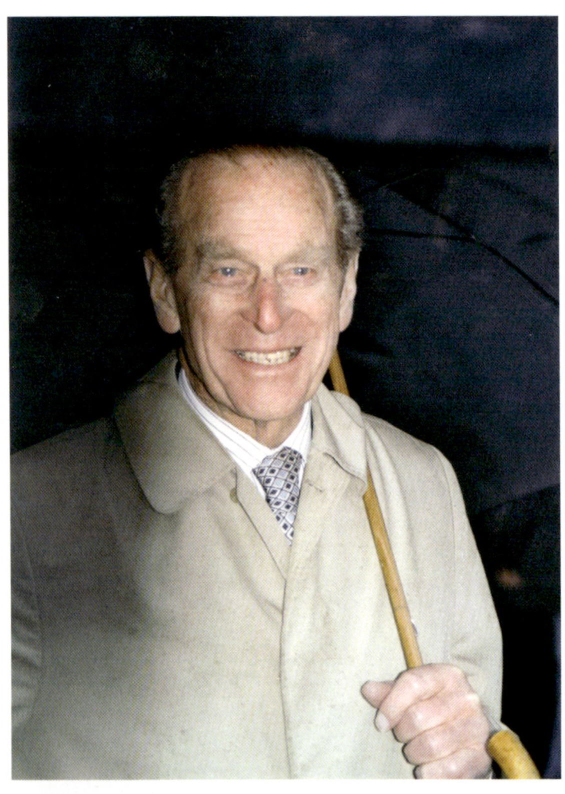

The Duke of Edinburgh, Chesterfield, November 2003
Clearly the wet weather has not affected the Duke's enthusiasm for the day's events.

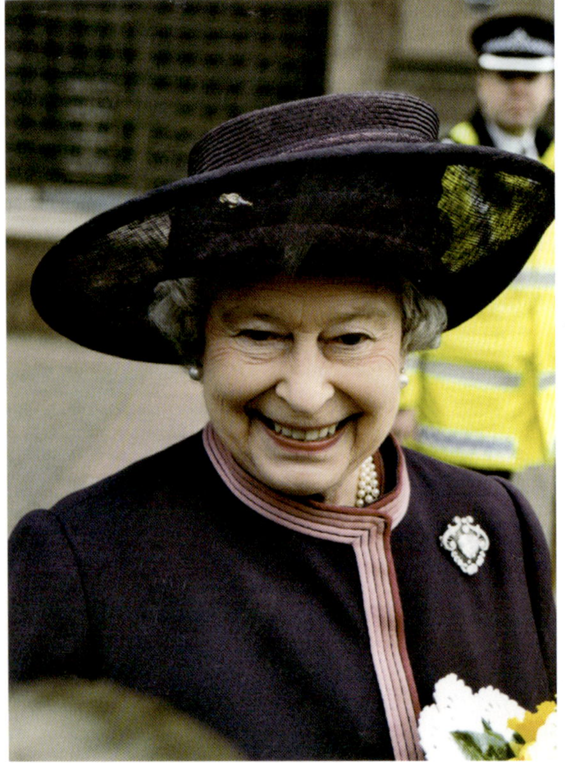

The Queen, Liverpool, 8 April 2004
The Royal Maundy this year was held in Liverpool. There, seventy-eight men and seventy-eight women (the number reflected the Queen's age) received two purses of Maundy money from her. The crowds had been much less for this visit than in previous years, but that didn't dampen the enthusiasm of the Queen for her people as she walked past them on her way to a reception in the Lady Chapel of Liverpool Cathedral.

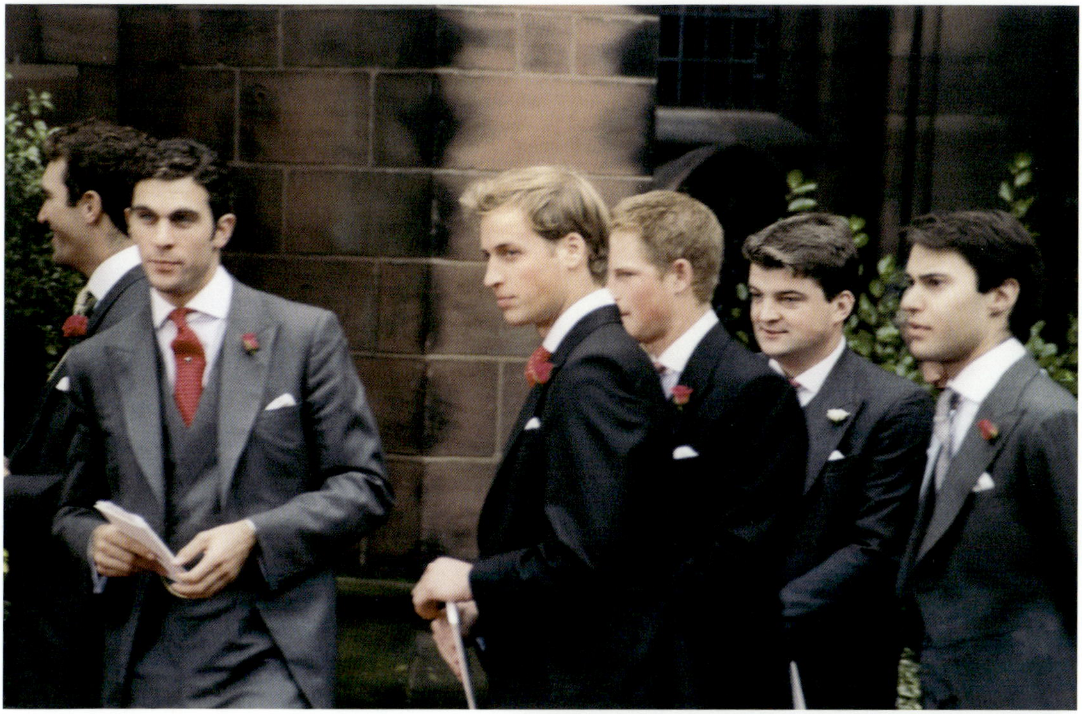

Princes William and Harry, Chester, November 2004

Attending the wedding of their great friends, Edward van Cutsem (once a pageboy at the 1981 wedding of their parents) and Lady Tamara Grosvenor (daughter of the Duke and Duchess of Westminster) were Princes William and Harry. The high-profile society wedding included the Queen and other Royals on the guest list; one notable absentee was Prince Charles. As the Royal Princes (who served as ushers) left the service, there were cries of 'Marry me, William!' from girls in the crowd, much to the amusement of the Princes. They were surrounded by the Van Cutsem family, and the lady in blue with Prince Harry is Lady Edwina Grosvenor.

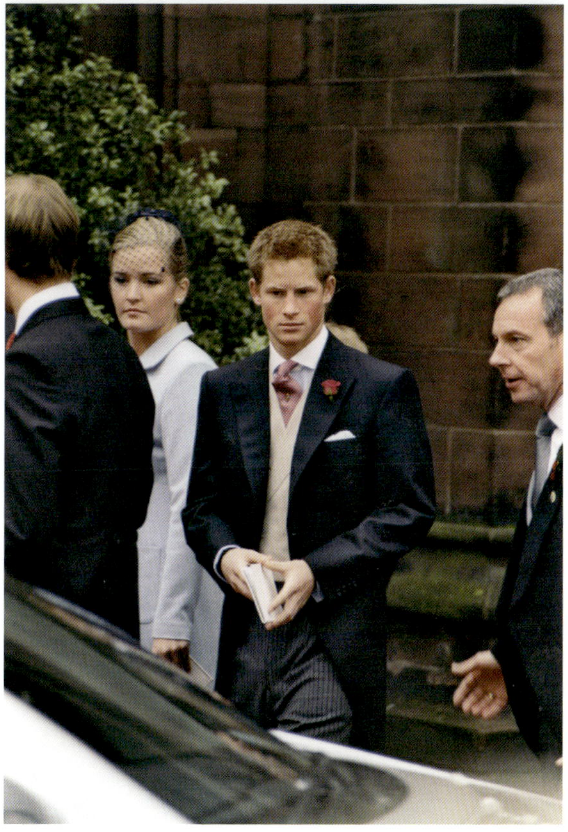

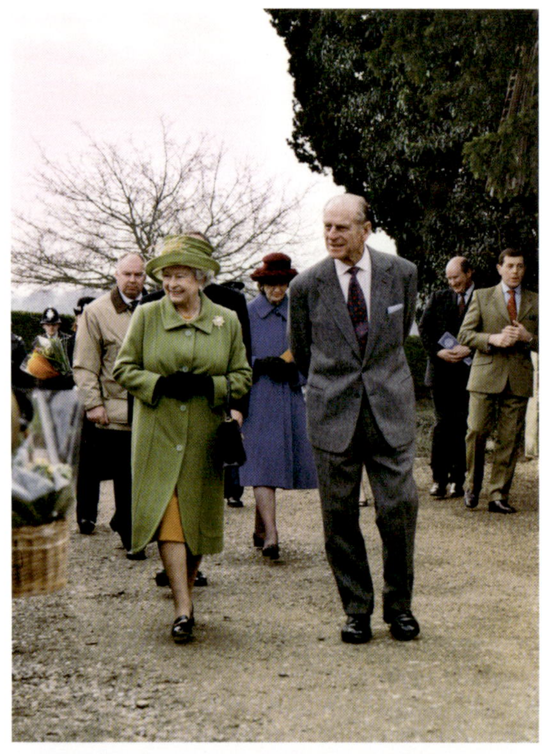

The Queen and the Duke of Edinburgh, West Newton, 6 February 2005
The Queen marked her accession to the throne forty-three years previously by attending morning service on the Sandringham Estate. Both she and the Duke, simply dressed in a tweed suit, walked up the driveway to the church hall.

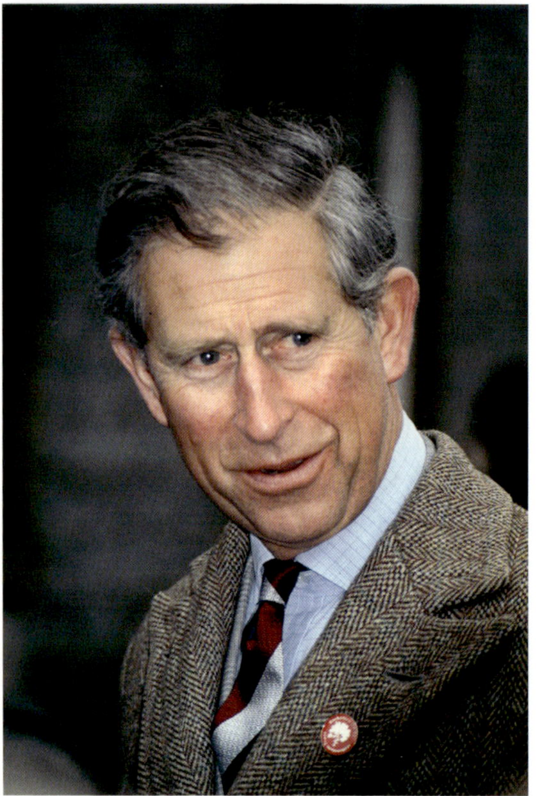

Prince Charles, Clapham, 22 March 2005
With his own wedding only a month away, the Prince visited the Yorkshire Dales, and came to Clapham. As Patron of the Yorkshire Dales Millennium Trust, he launched a £1 million 'Donate to the Dales' appeal. Through the narrow streets of the village, large numbers turned out to see him as he walked around on his tour.

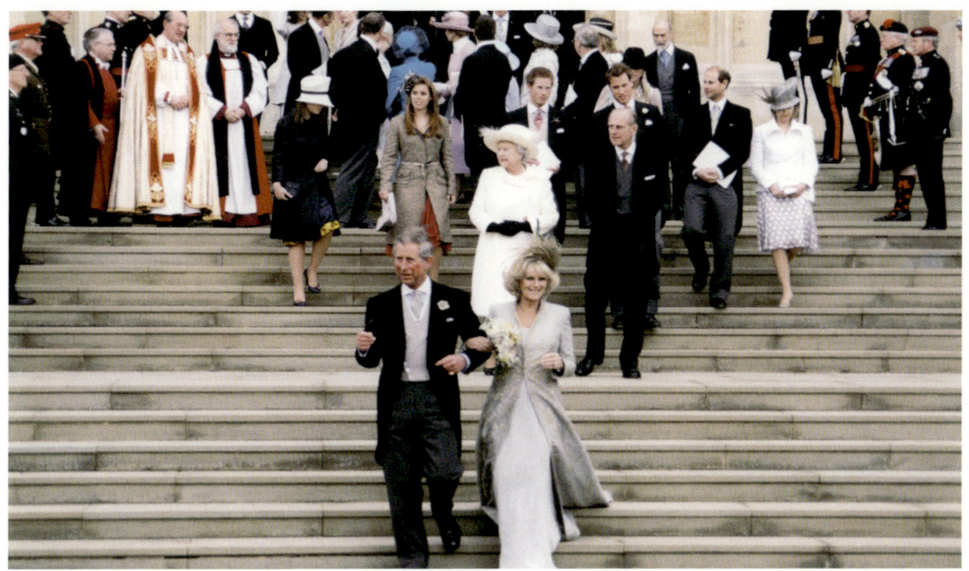

Charles and Camilla's Wedding, Windsor, April 2005

It had been a day that many had awaited, and indeed this Royal wedding had its fair share of disasters along the way – the most notable being the change in date following the death of Pope John Paul II. Windsor, always a favourite with the Royal Family, was the location. After the wedding at the Guildhall on Windsor's High Street, a service of prayer and dedication followed in St George's Chapel. I was lucky to have an amazing view from within the Horseshoe Cloister, and the opportunity to see the newly-married Prince and Duchess of Cornwall, alongside their family, is something I will never forget.

As they descended the stone steps, a guard of honour formed from the various regiments the Prince is connected with lining their way and his immediate family followed. Then as the Royal couple went walkabout amongst their friends, guests and charities, the Royal Family and Parker Bowles family waited for their cars, and in the days of modern transport – minibuses!

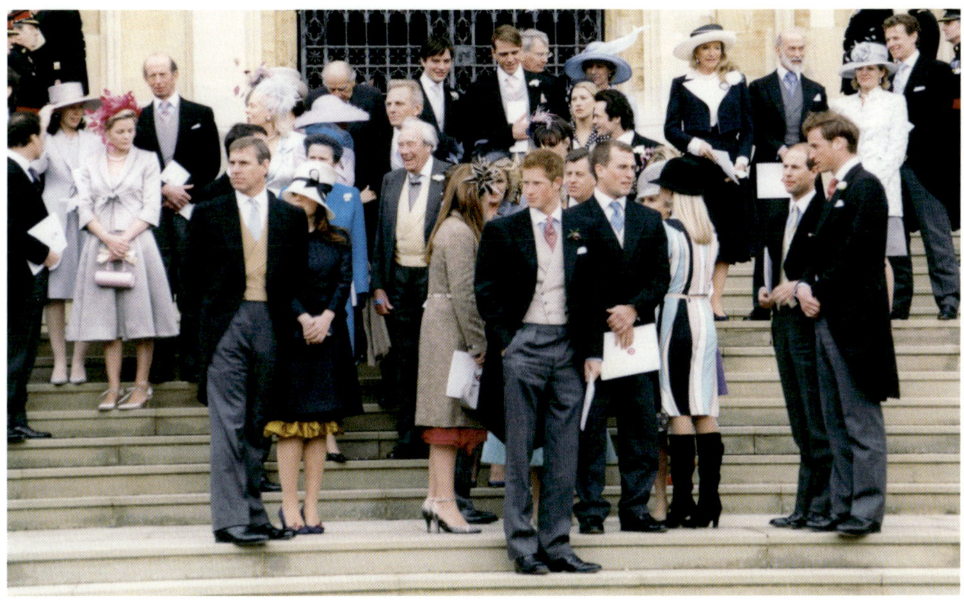

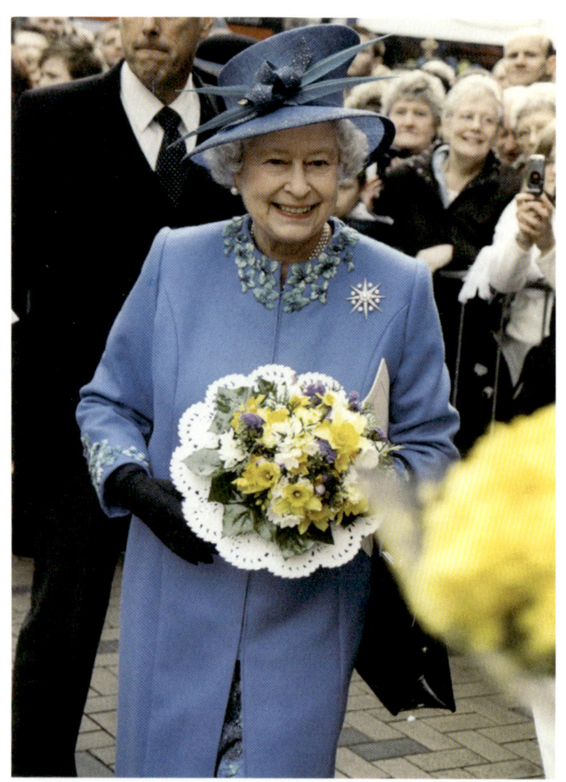

Left:
The Queen, Royal Maundy, Wakefield, March 2005
Dressed in bright blue – with the silver thread from her hat reflecting in the spring sunshine, the Queen delighted the crowds with an informal walkabout after the Royal Maundy service in Wakefield's cathedral.

Below and opposite:
Trooping the Colour, London, June 2005
Princesses Beatrice and Eugenie were given a prime seat in the second carriage as they were driven, along with their father, Prince Andrew, back to Buckingham Palace. Following behind were their grandparents, the Queen and Duke of Edinburgh. Also on the balcony for the first time was Camilla, Duchess of Cornwall (wearing the outfit she had worn to the Guildhall on her wedding day), as they all waved to the large crowds thronged at the palace gates.

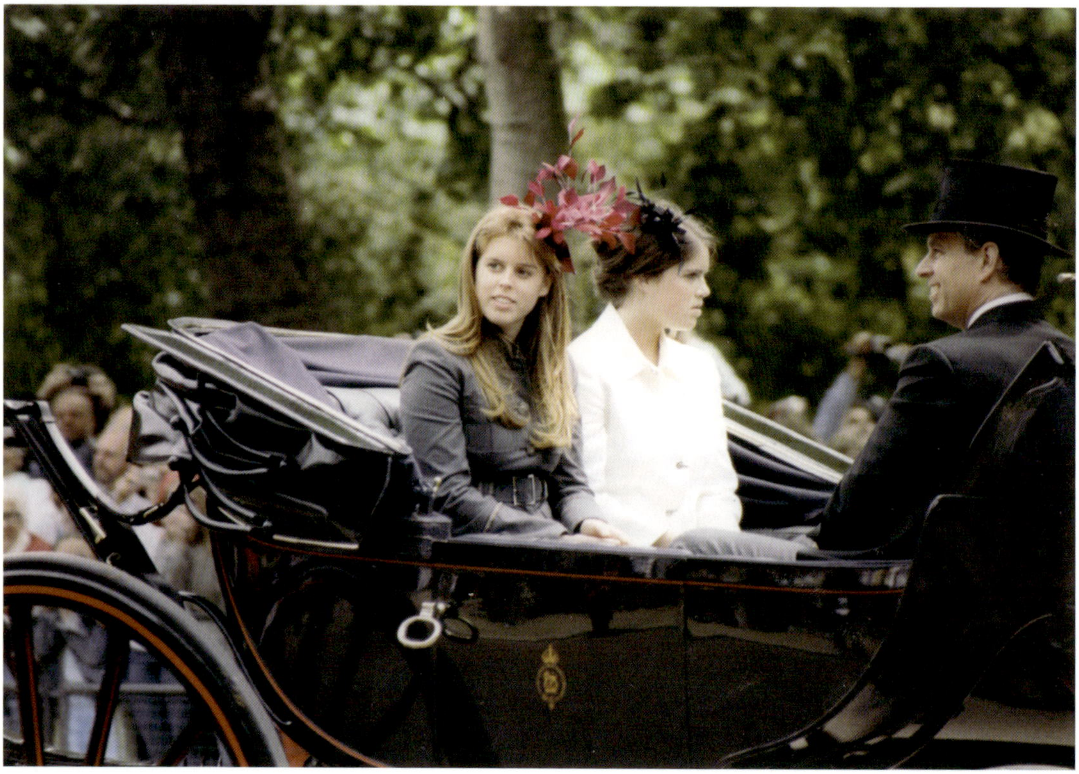

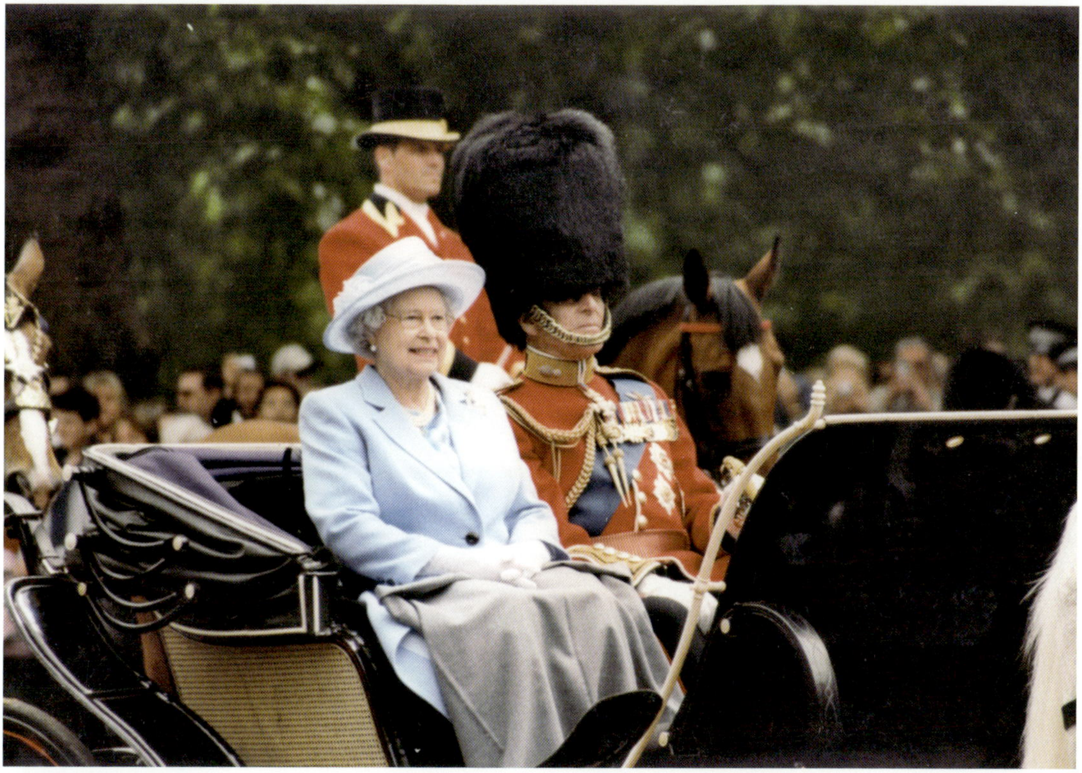

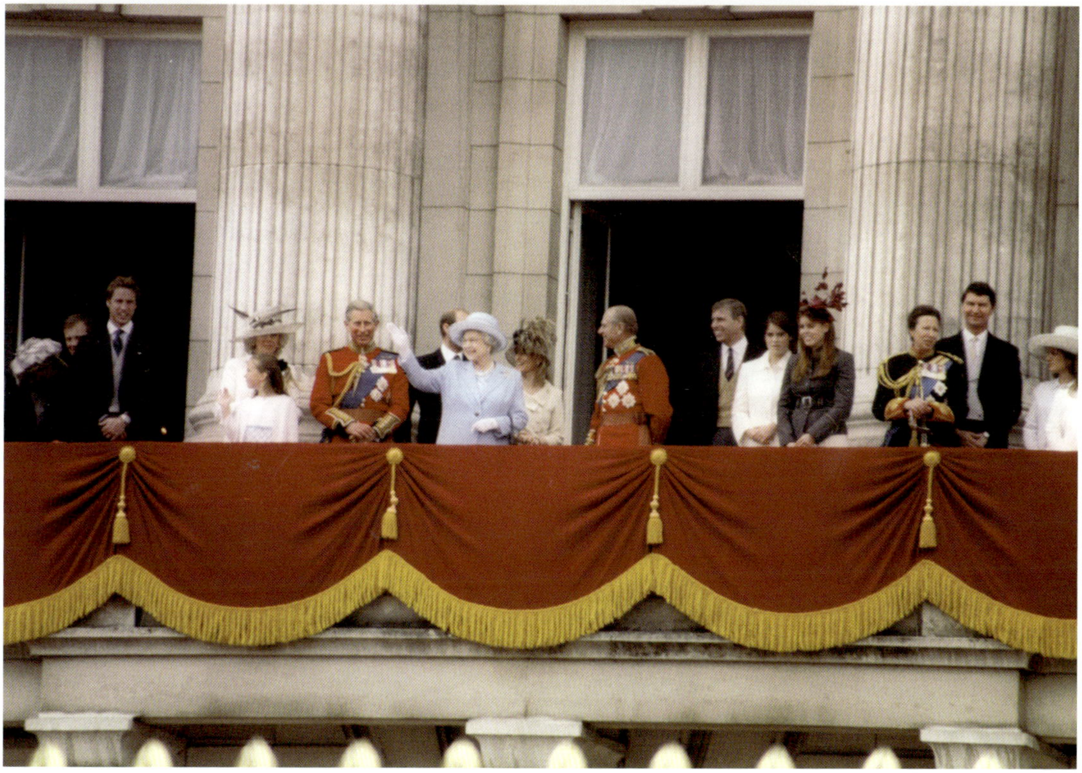

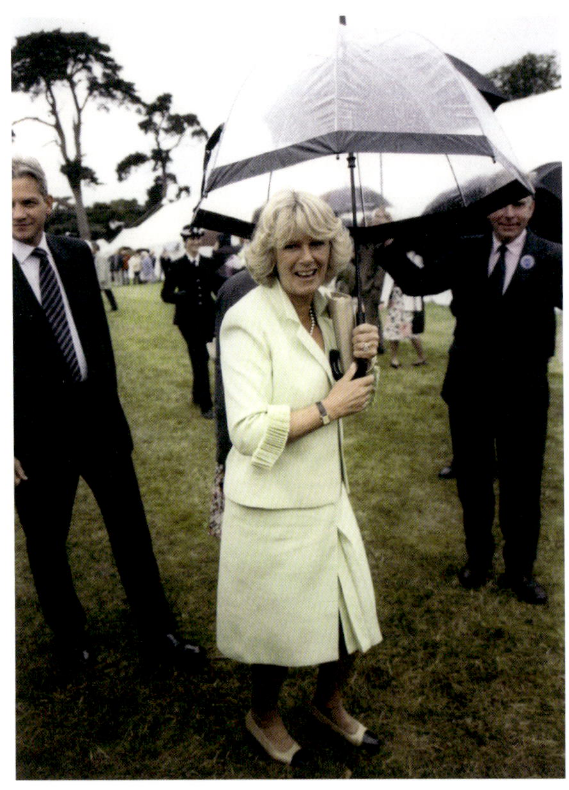

It's been called Britain's largest village fête, and every year was attended by the Queen Mother, along with Prince Charles. Since his grandmother's death, the Prince had continued that tradition, and this year his new wife was at his side. Her relaxed and informal manner soon won her friends as she made everyone feel at ease. However, the use of umbrellas only added to the regal feel, as the Duchess used a transparent one so favoured by other Royal ladies.

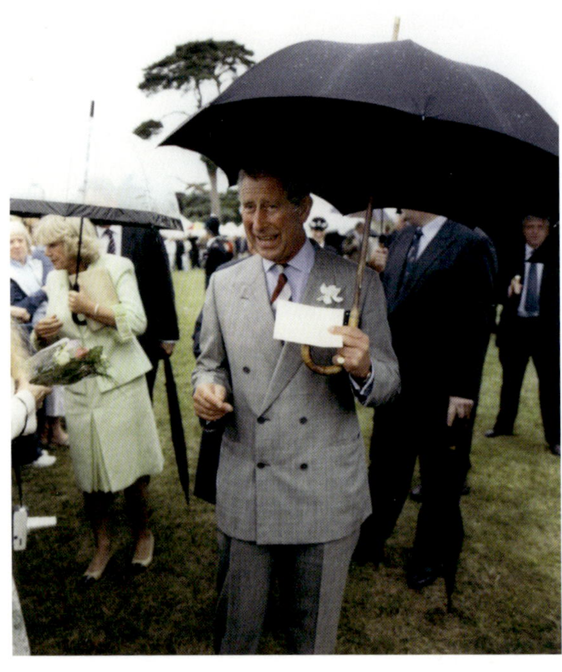

Sophie, Countess of Wessex, Wakefield, 18 October 2005

The Countess, as patron of Mencap, visited the 'Your Voice, Wakefield Advocacy' project at the city's town hall. Celebrating its third anniversary, the Countess met some of the local people the charity help.

Prince Charles, Nelson, October 2005

Prince Charles toured the area of Nelson, to see for himself at first hand all the regeneration that had commenced in his capacity as president of the Prince's Foundation for the Built Environment. As he left St Mary's church, he managed a few words of thanks for a local policeman on duty.

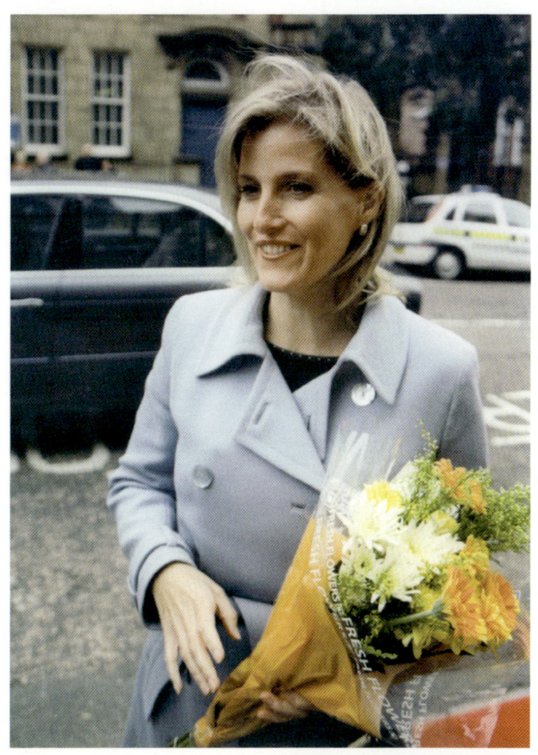

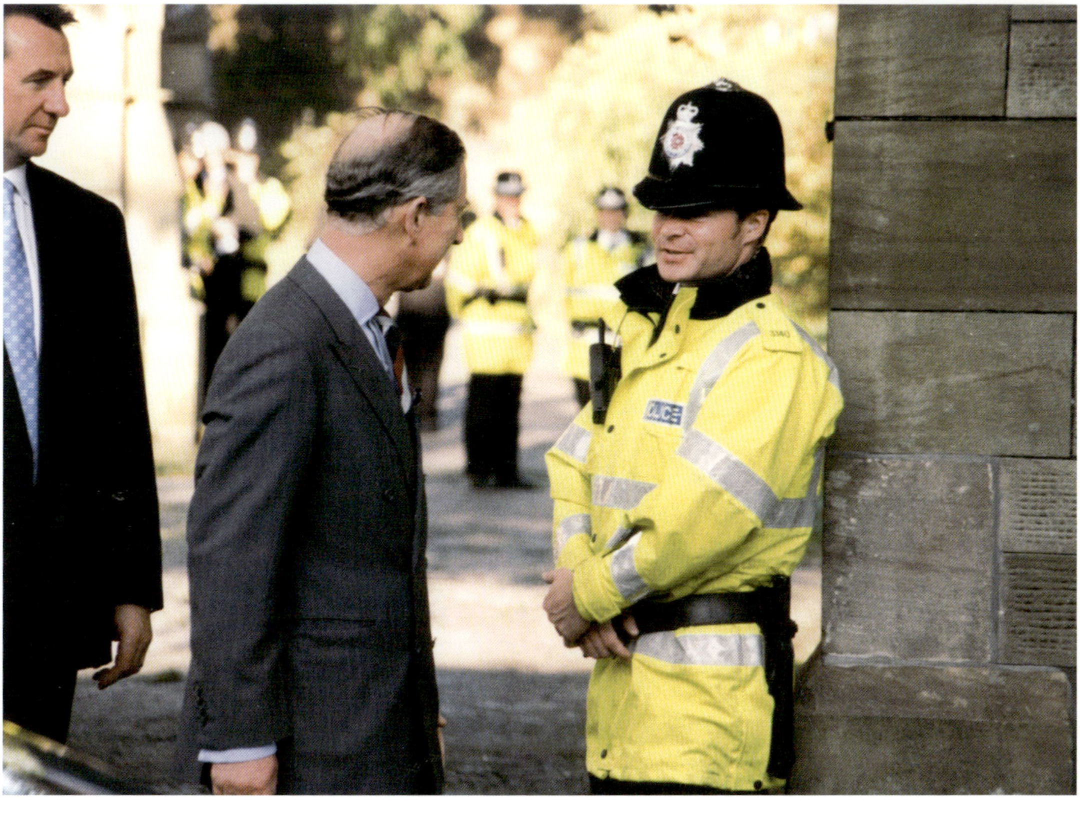

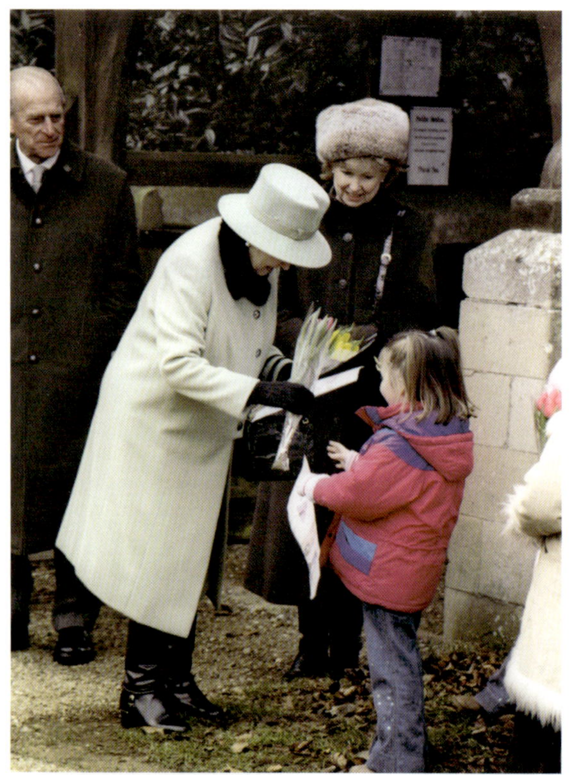

The Queen, Wolverton, January 2006
While her husband stood in the background, the Queen accepted flowers from a little girl outside the Church of St Peter in Wolverton, Norfolk. The Queen was warmly wrapped up in a fur scarf and boots for the winter weather.

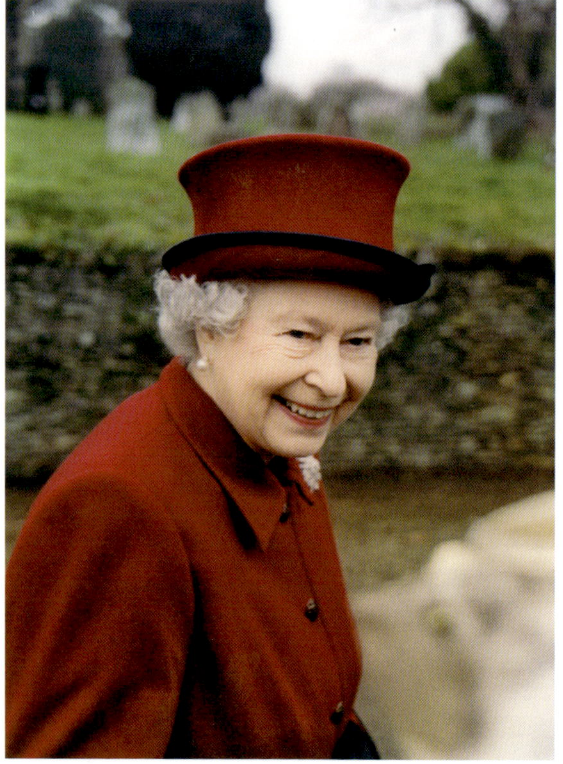

The Queen, West Newton, 5 February 2006
A few weeks later, the Queen was saying goodbye to Norfolk on her traditional attendance at church. And it was back to London for the Royal party to re-commence state business, and Royal duties.

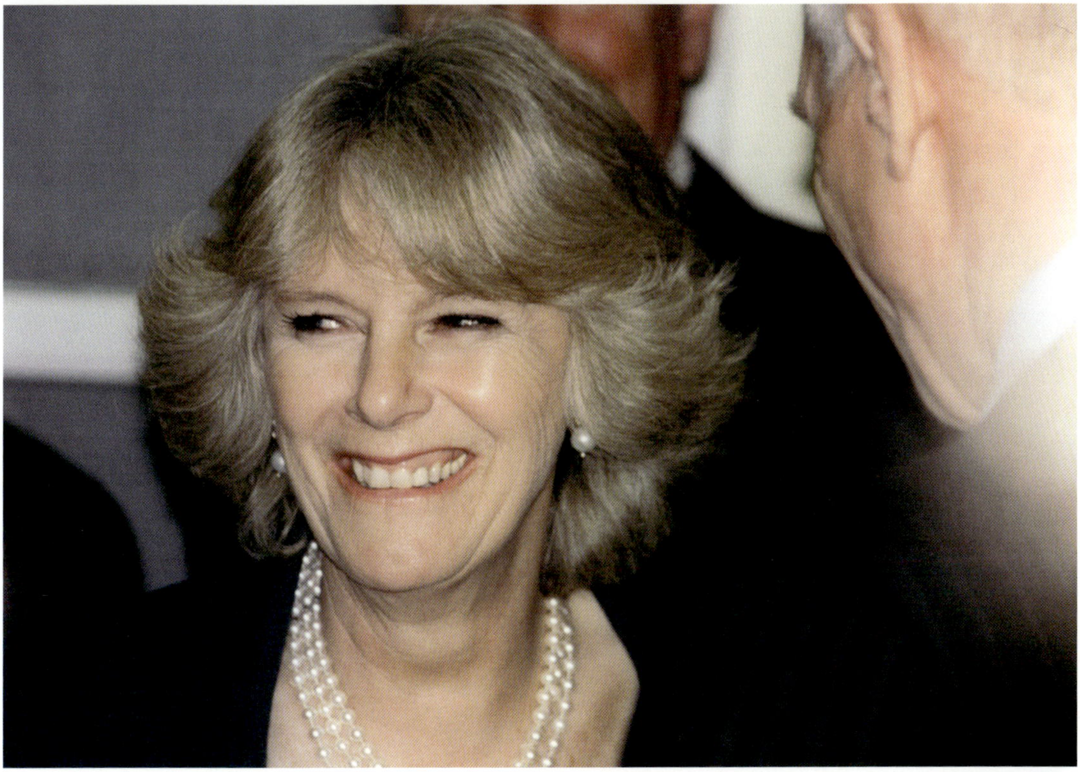

**The Duchess of Cornwall, Hull,
7 February 2006**

Arriving at the Centre for Metabolic Bone
Disease at Hull's Royal Infirmary was the
Duchess of Cornwall. Her visit was to
raise awareness of osteoporosis, a disease
that had affected her own mother and
grandmother. From there, it was onto the
Age Concern Healthy Living Centre, where
she met volunteers in the shop and even
had time for a cup of tea with supporters.

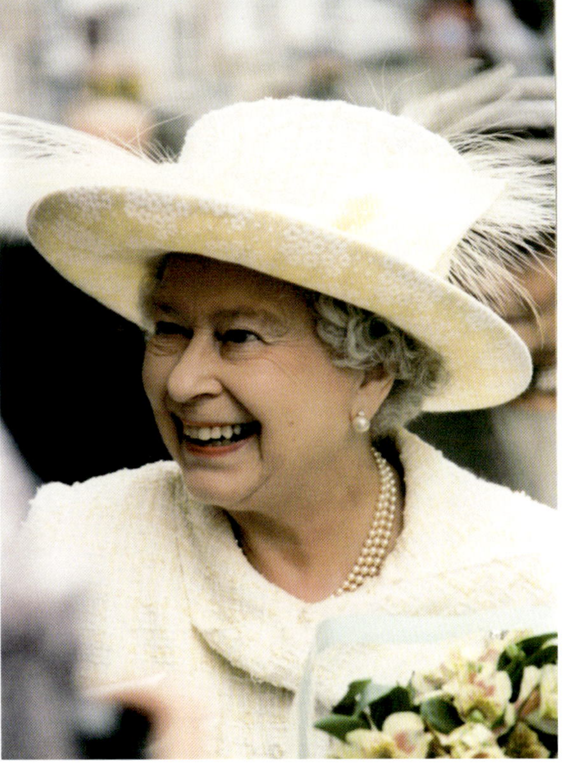

Right:

The Queen, Guildford, 13 April 2006

Having arrived earlier to visit Guildford's
cathedral for the Royal Maundy
ceremony, the Queen and Duke made
their way up the cobbled High Street
to attend a lunch at the town hall. Vast
crowds thronged every vantage point
as the Queen took her time receiving
handful after handful of bouquets.
Showing her frugal side, she even wore
the outfit seen the previous year at Prince
Charles' wedding.

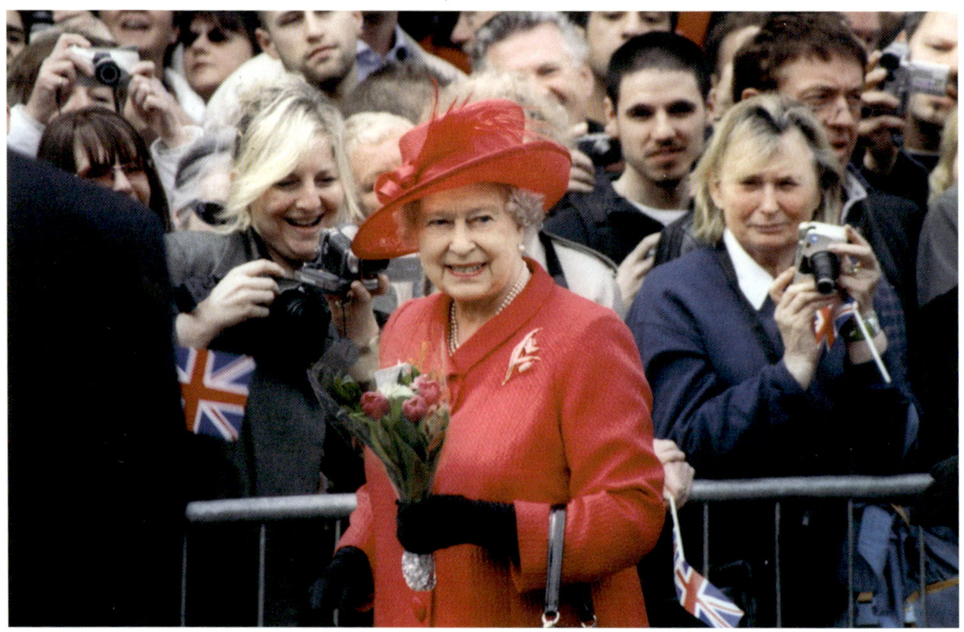

The Queen, Windsor, 21 April 2006

Celebrating her eightieth birthday, the Queen chose her favourite home, Windsor Castle. At times there were more press than public, but as is the case with many Royal events, the numbers increase as the minutes decrease! When the clocks struck 11 a.m., and she appeared at the Henry VIII Gateway to meet representatives of youth organisations, Windsor's narrow streets were fit to bursting! Slowly, she walked down toward the statue of Queen Victoria. Showing her charismatic diplomatic silence, when I asked, 'Your Majesty, what is the secret of your great stamina?' she simply smiled and said, 'I don't know!' With the Duke by her side, she walked along the High Street to her waiting car, the boot filled with floral tributes, cards and gifts. It had indeed been a memorable day for her.

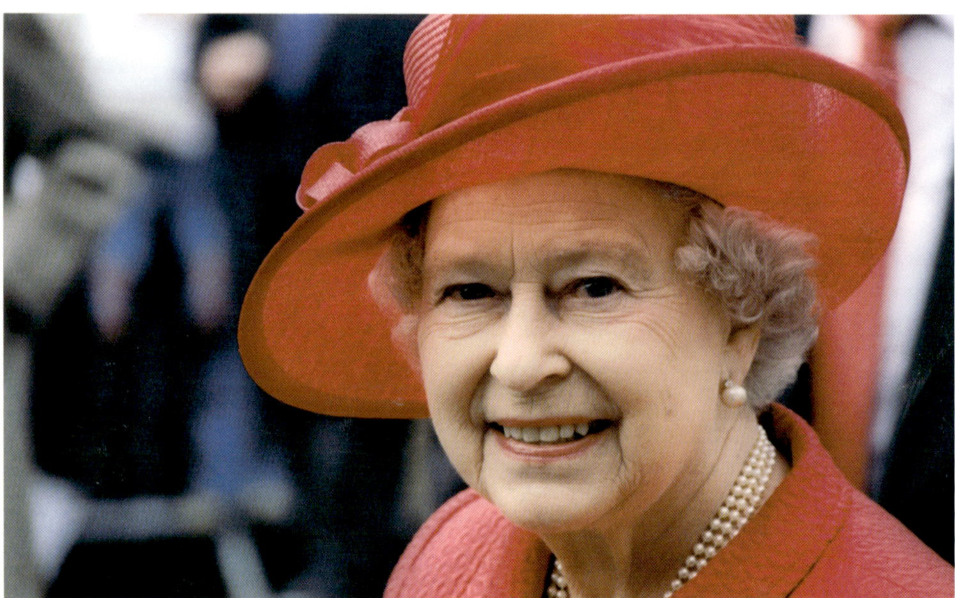

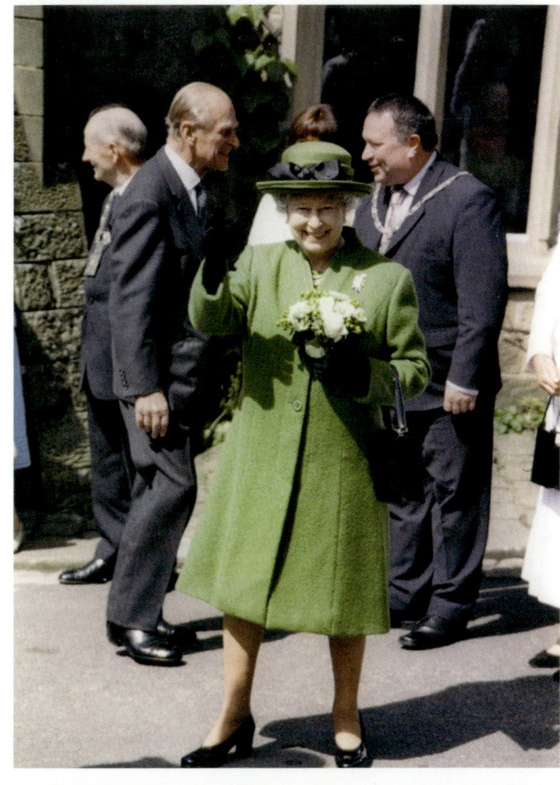

The Queen and the Duke of Edinburgh, Whitewell, May 2006

Visiting the Duchy of Lancaster estates (after a morning visit to Blackburn), the Queen had her first pub lunch at The Inn at Whitewell, hosted by the Council of the Duchy of Lancaster. Previously she was quoted in the press as saying she would, if she ever retired, settle in the Ribble Valley, and I truly agree that the scenery and countryside was breathtaking. After she ate cottage pie, apple crumble tart and Lancashire cheeses, she waved at onlookers, before she and the Prince got into separate Land Rovers to travel onto their next engagements.

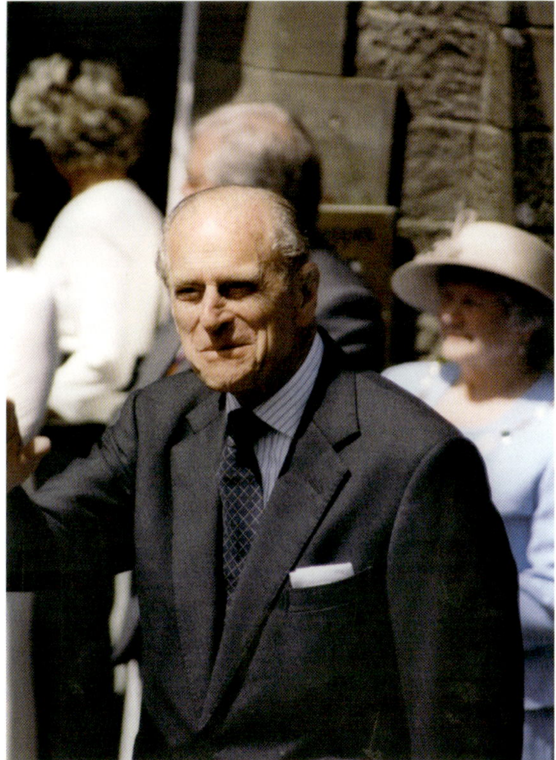

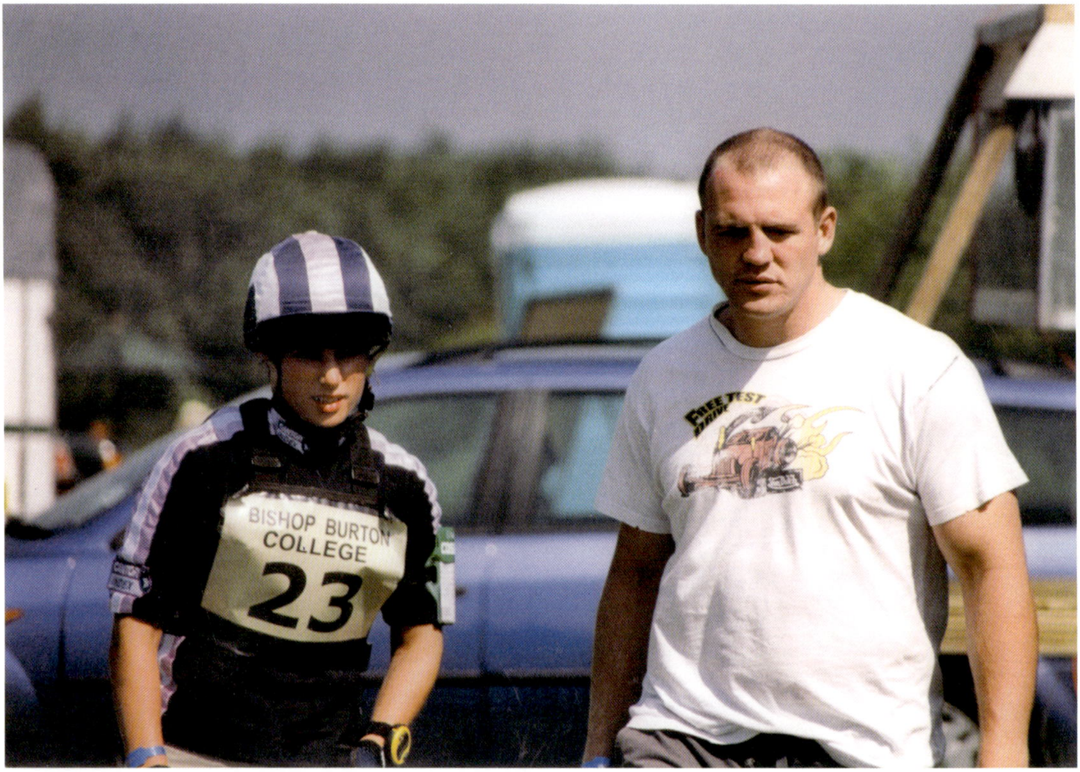

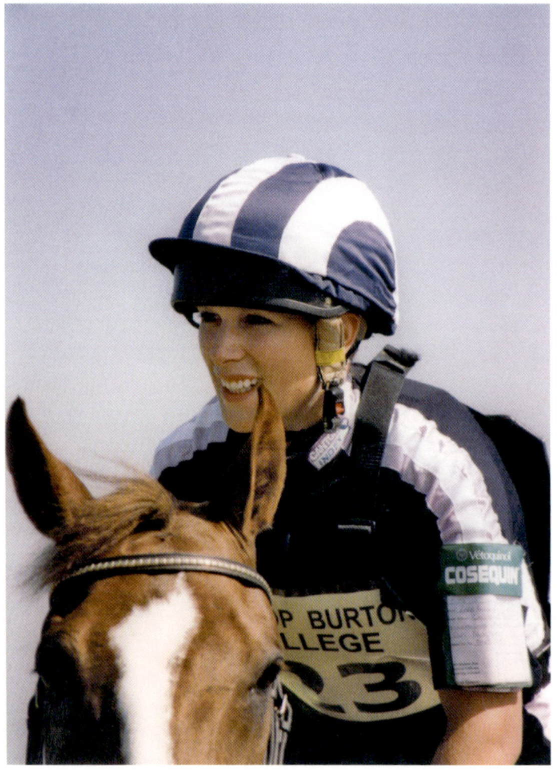

Zara Phillips and Mike Tindall, Bramham, June 2006

As the daughter of Princess Anne, Zara Phillips' appearances are limited to family occasions; however, like her mother, she is an accomplished horsewoman. She competed in the Bramham International Horse Trials on the outskirts of Leeds. Rather touchingly, her boyfriend Mike Tindall (now her fiancé) accompanied her and was helping her with the horse, and also fetching her water. Zara's skills are legendary in equestrian circles and she has gone onto achieve a great deal.

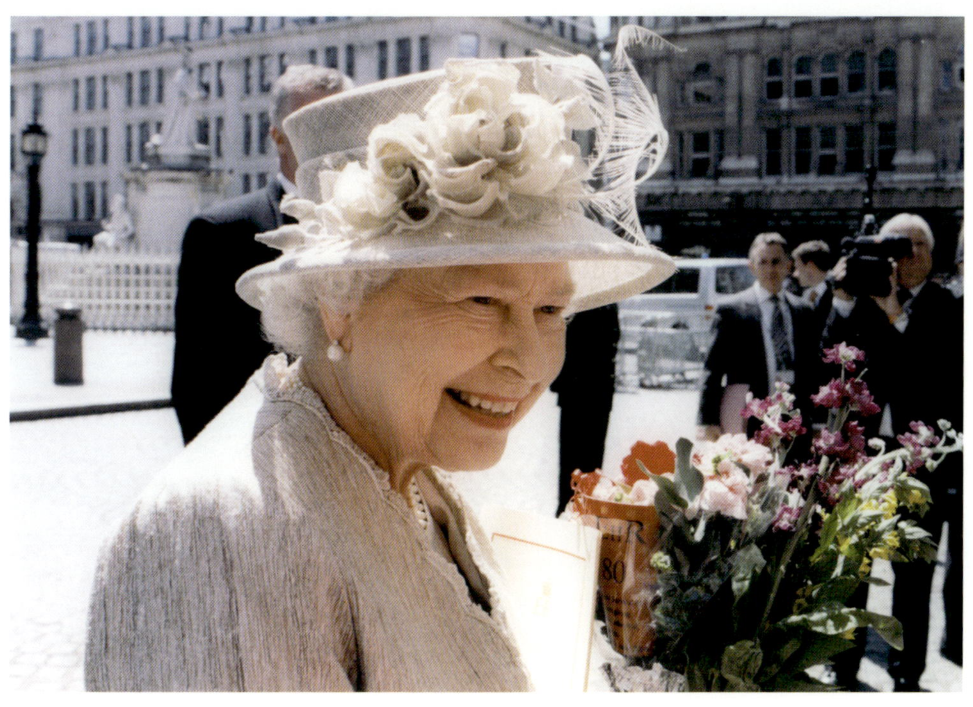

The Queen's Eightieth Birthday Service, London, 15 June 2006

After celebrating her eightieth birthday in April, the Queen was surrounded by her family as they attended a service of thanksgiving for her birthday at London's St Paul's Cathedral. With her grandchildren and children on the steps of the cathedral, the Queen went walkabout in the June sunshine.

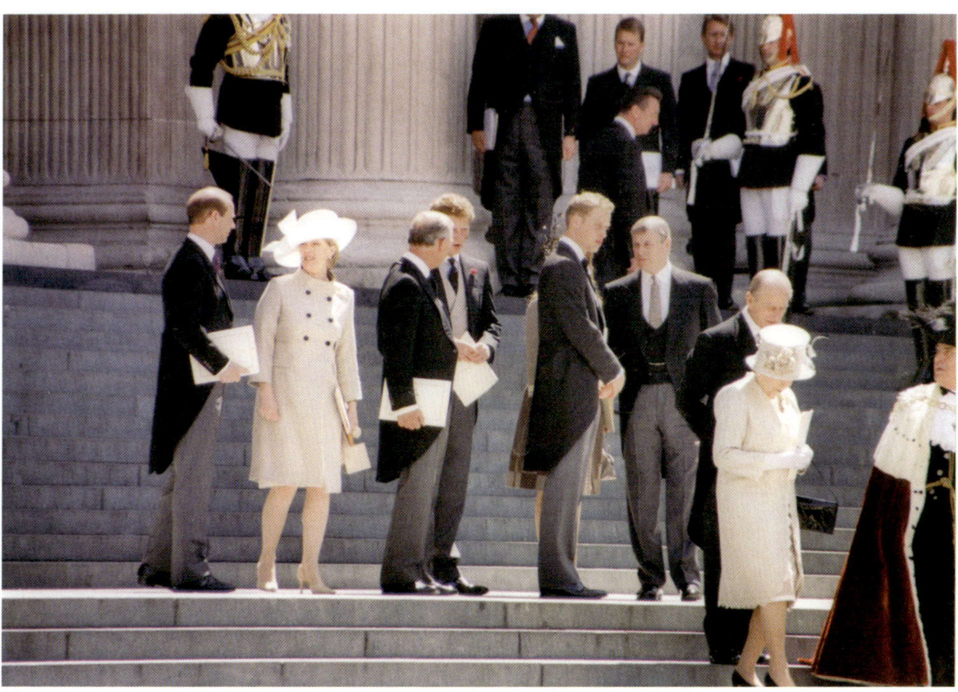

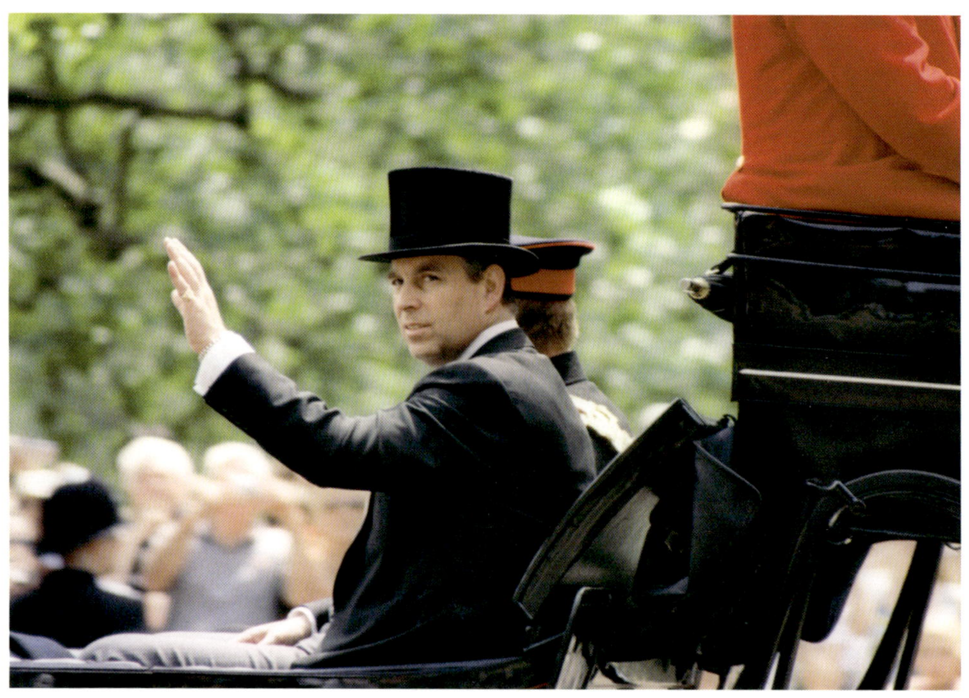

Trooping the Colour, London, June 2006
This year's Trooping the Colour was a little special; watching from the balcony, the Queen and the Royal Family watched a 'Feu de Joie' (Fire of Joy), when the guardsmen fired into the sky – a special gesture in this eightieth birthday year, it proved to be a rather smokey one too!

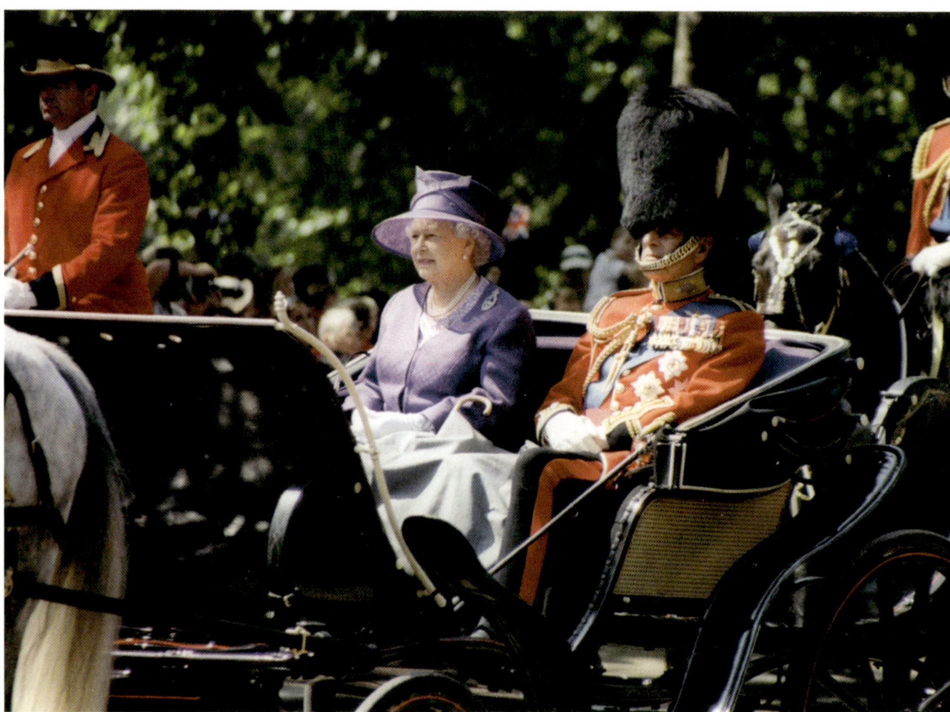

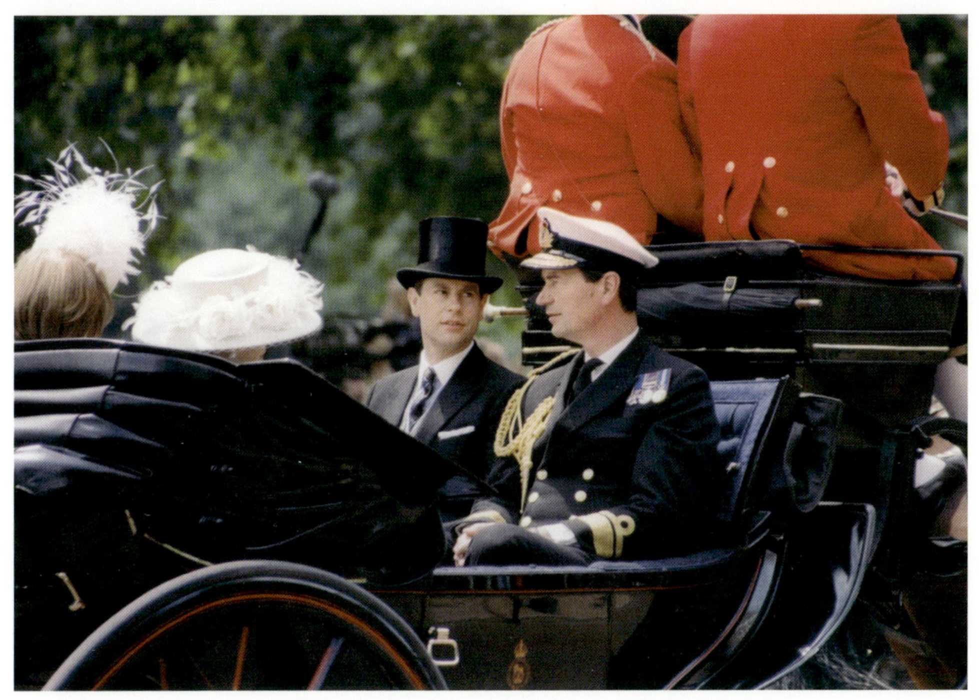

Prince Edward sits next to Princess Anne's husband, Commander Timothy Laurence.

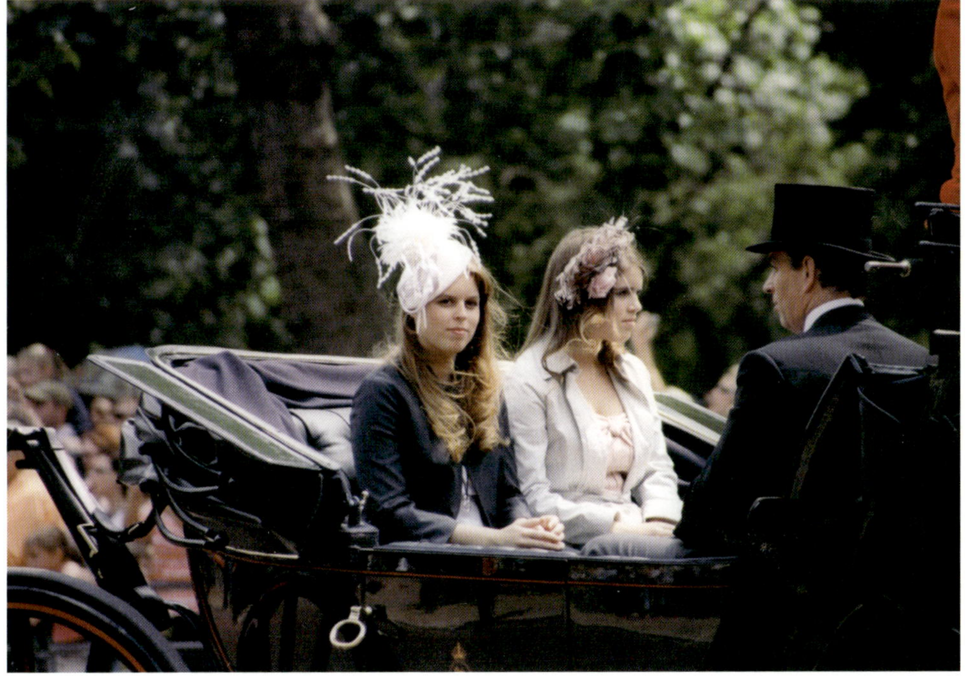

Princesses Beatrice and Eugenie, dressed very smartly for the occasion.

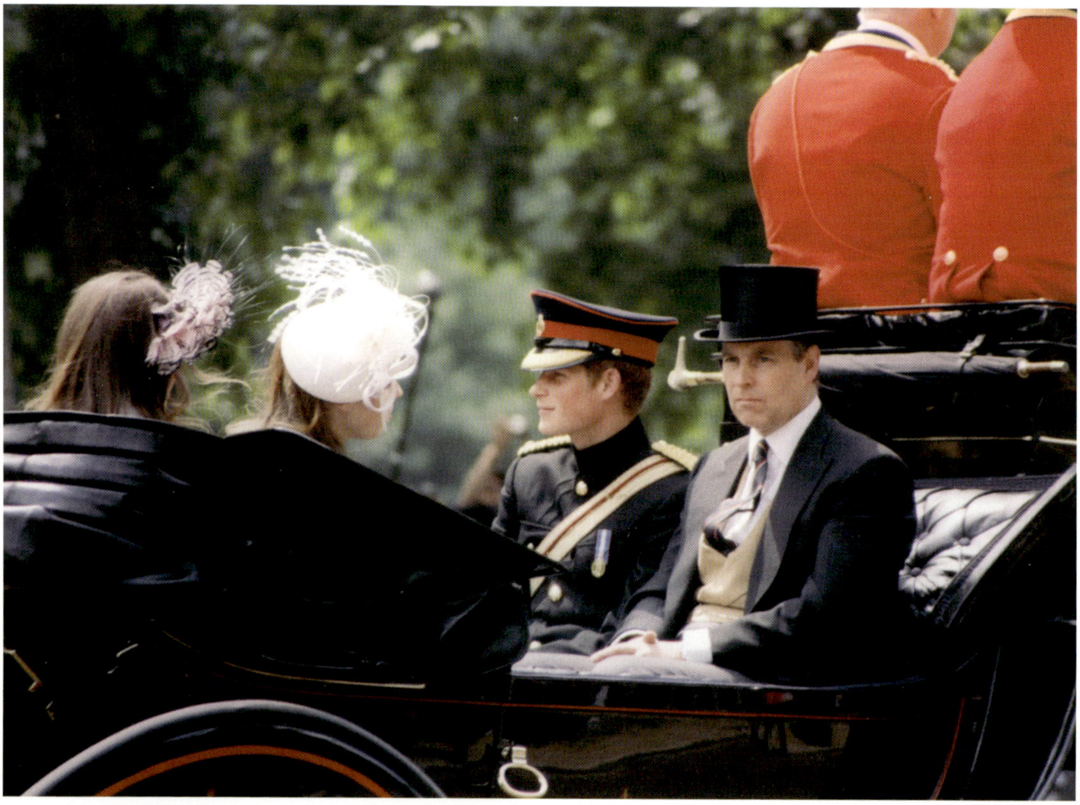

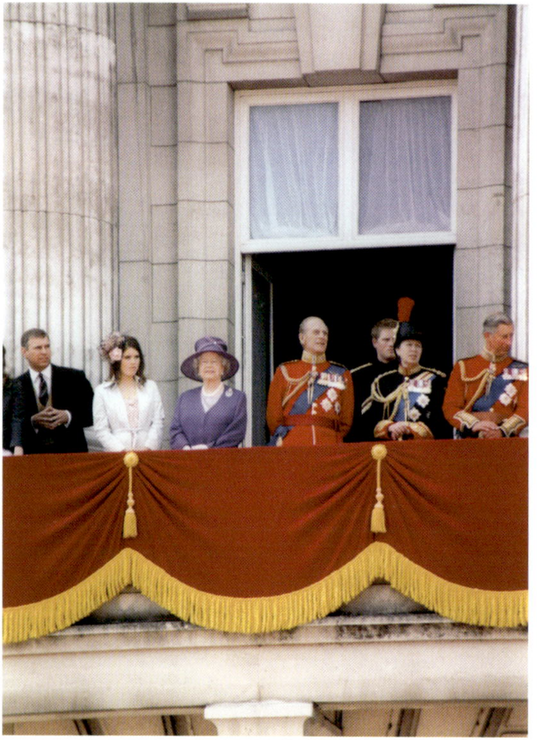

Trooping the Colour, June 2006
Princes Harry and Andrew.

Left:
**The balcony of Buckingham Palace,
following the Trooping of the Colour,
June 2006.**
From left to right: Prince Andrew, Princess
Eugenie, Her Majesty the Queen, the Duke
of Edinburgh, Prince Harry, Princess Anne
and Prince Charles.

Right:
Prince Charles and the Duchess of Cornwall, Sandringham, July 2006
'It's hotter in there than some of the overseas tours I've been on', the Prince joked as he left the Flower Marquee. Temperatures soared at this year's Sandringham Flower Show, with all visitors trying their best to keep cool in the sunshine – the Royal couple included. The Duchess was overheard to say, 'I'm sweltering in the heat.'

Below:
Her Majesty the Queen, Manchester, April 2007
The site of the Royal Maundy this year was chosen as Manchester Cathedral. After the official photocall, the Royal party made their way to Chetham's School of Music, stopping along the way to chat with the crowds.

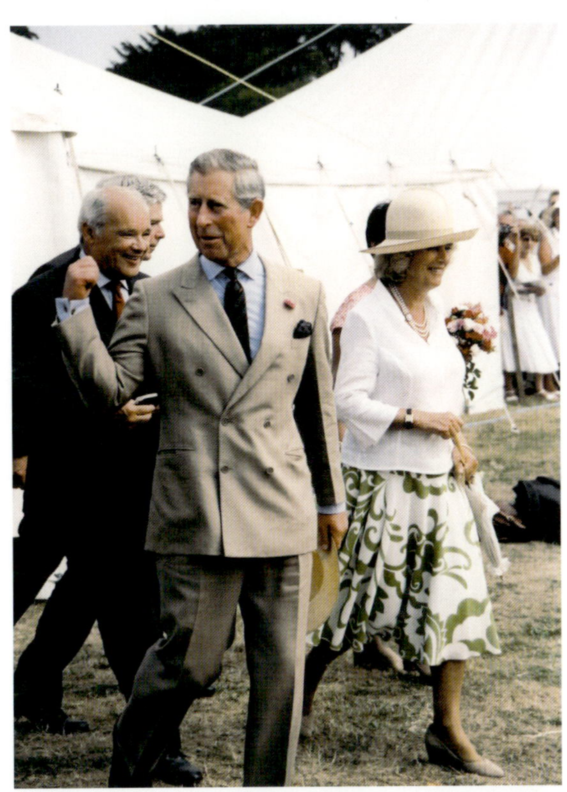

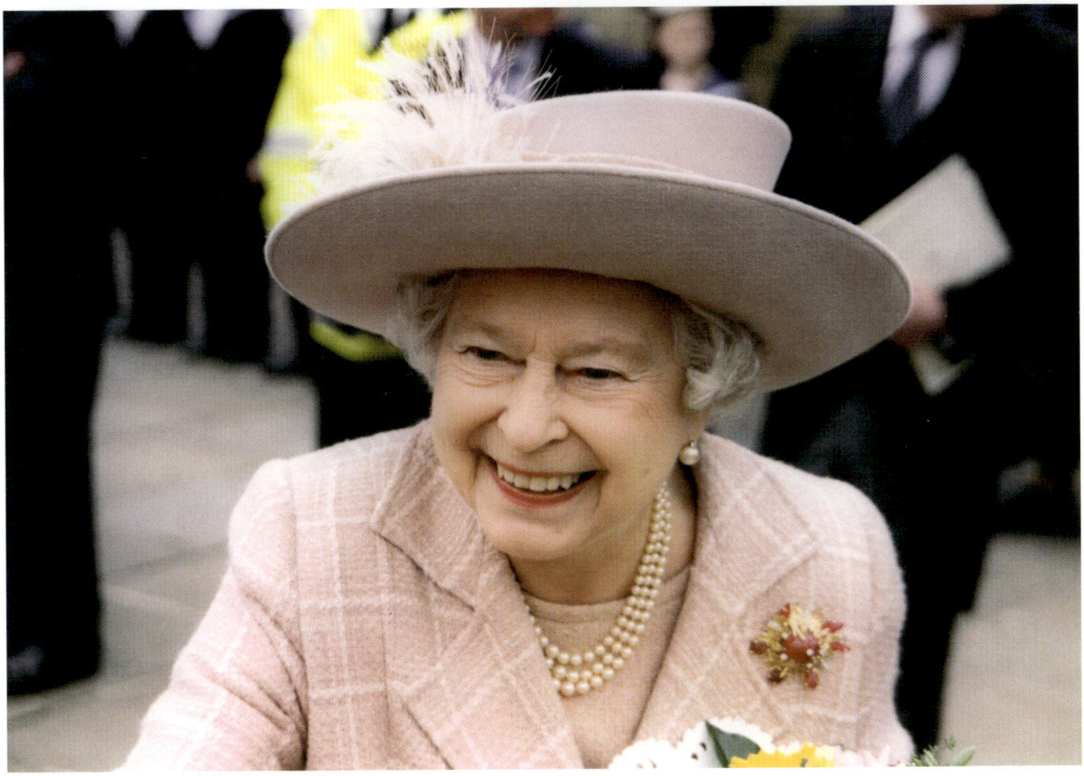

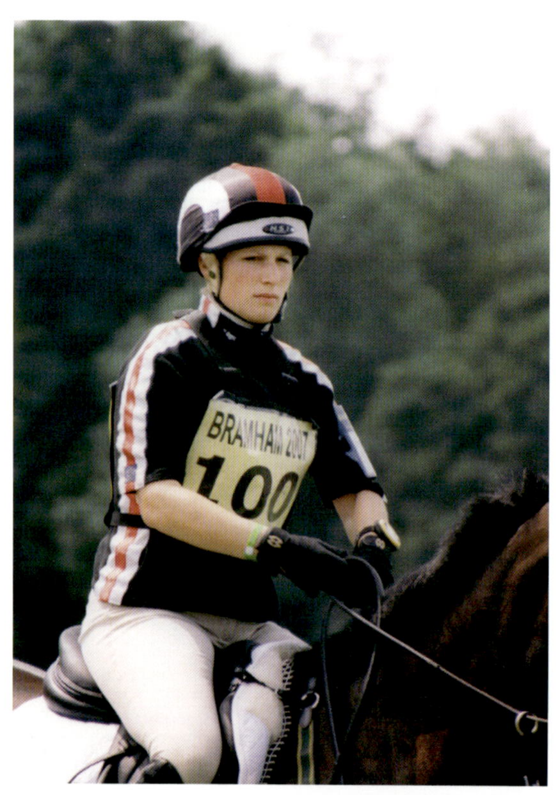

Left:

Zara Phillips, Bramham, June 2007
Sadly for Zara Phillips, her attendance at this Branham Horse Show wasn't to bode very well, as her horse fell after several obstacles. The young Royal, however, showed her true spirit and remained calm.

Below:

Her Majesty the Queen and the Duke of Edinburgh, the Garter Ceremony, June 2007
The Queen and Duke rode back in one of the Ascot carriages after leaving the service for the Order of the Garter. As soon as they came into view, a large cheer erupted from within the Castle walls.

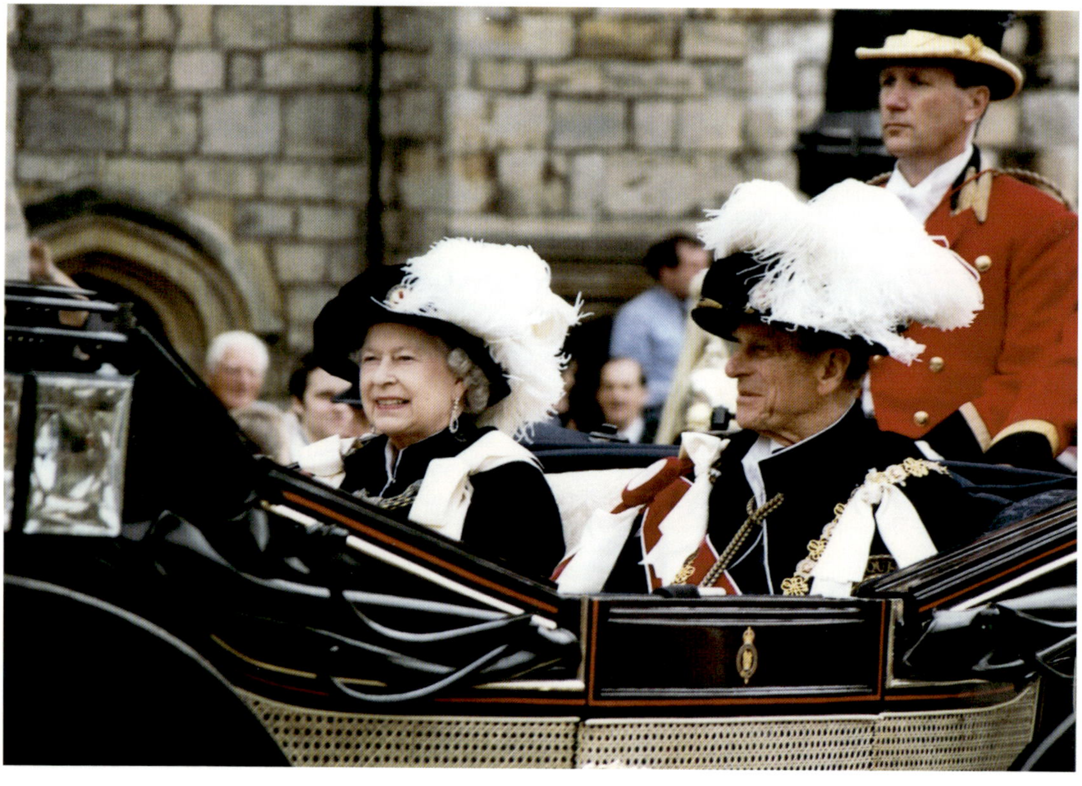

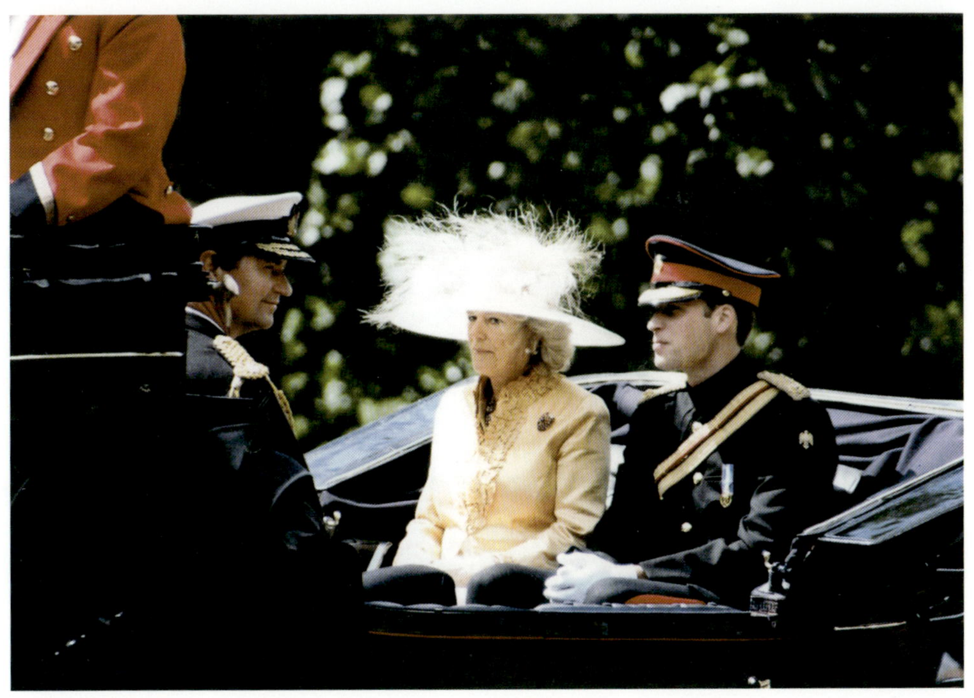

Trooping the Colour, London, June 2007

Wearing an amazing hat trimmed with feathers, the Duchess of Cornwall sat next to her stepson Prince William in the carriage procession. Later on, a few of the youngest members of the Queen's family joined her on the balcony, including the young children of her nephew, Viscount Linley – the son of the late Princess Margaret.

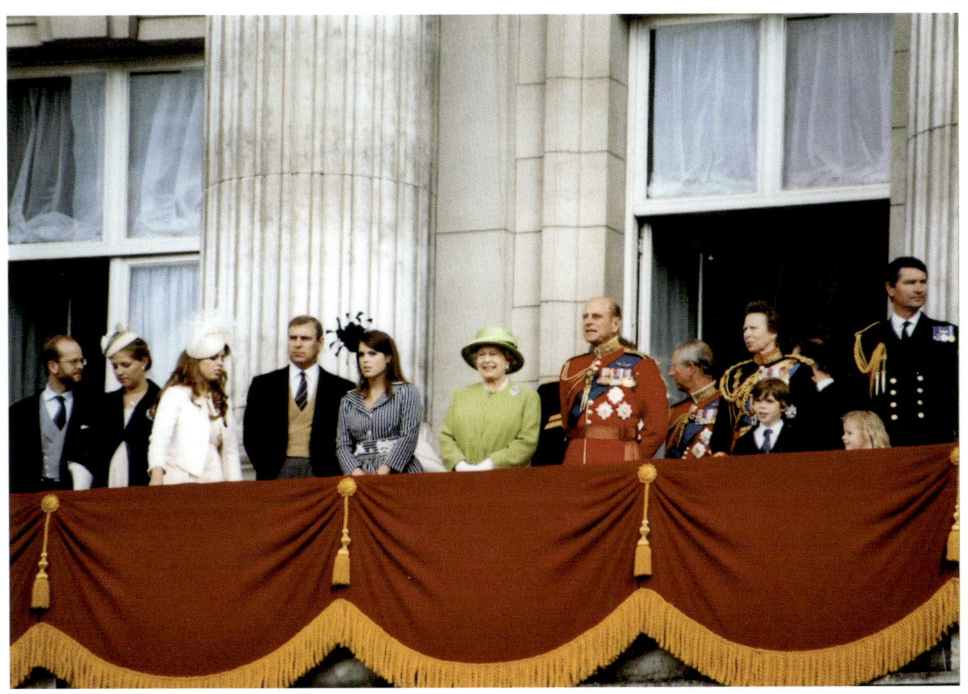

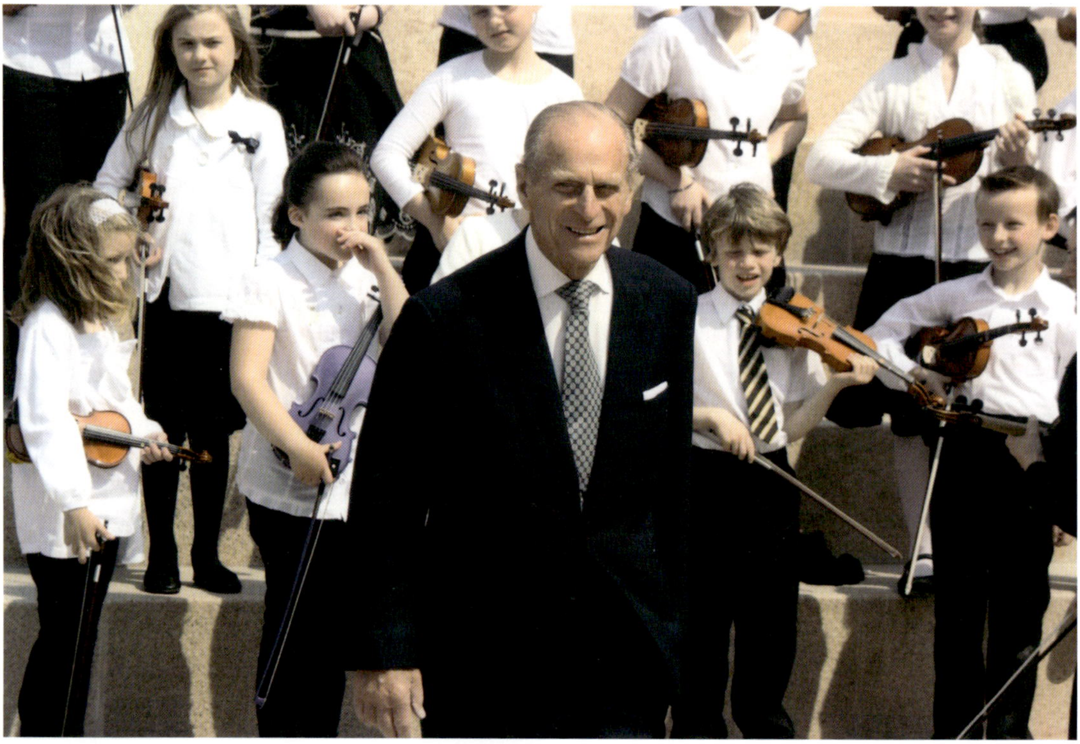

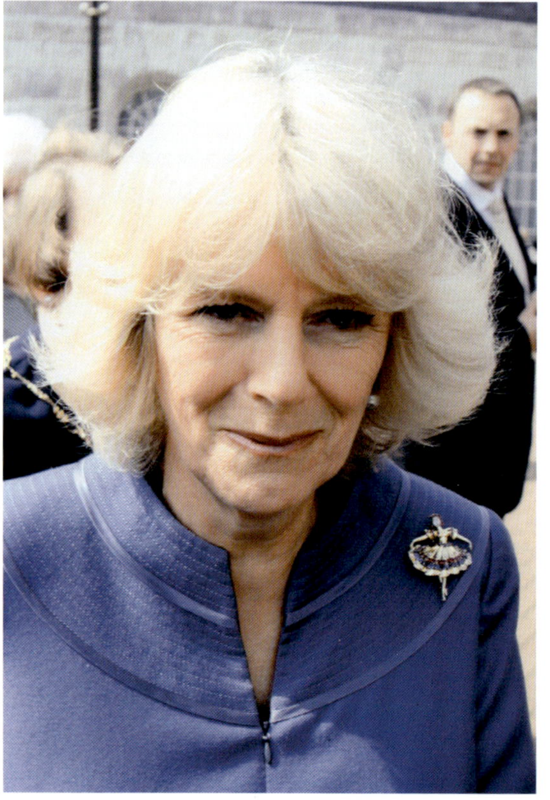

Above:

The Duke of Edinburgh, Liverpool, May 2008

Having officially visited the new Liverpool One retail quarter, Prince Philip was serenaded by a band of young violinists as he walked past. He made a point of going up to them for a chat, and showed great delight in their accomplishments.

Left:

The Duchess of Cornwall, Birmingham, 22 April 2008

After opening the town hall with the Prince of Wales, the Duchess attended a fundraising lunch for a local ballet company; on her dress, she wears, appropriately, a ballerina brooch.

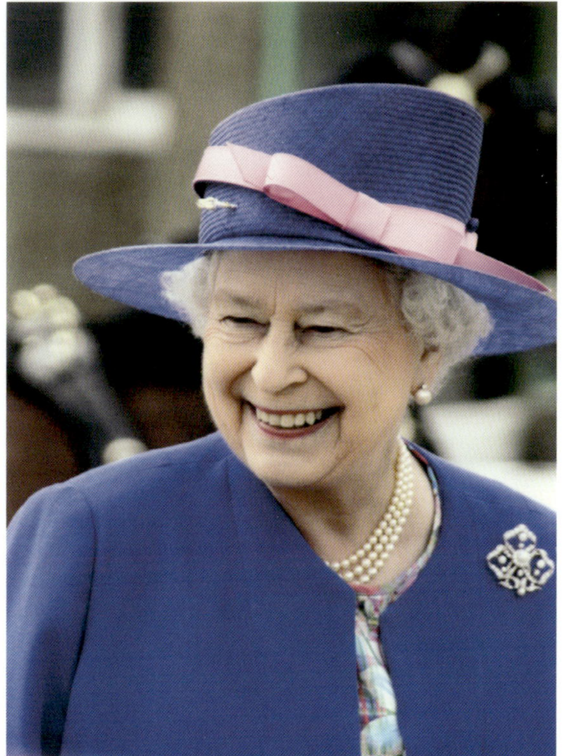

The Queen and the Duke of Edinburgh, Harrogate, July 2008

The Great Yorkshire Show in Harrogate welcomed two very special visitors to mark its 150th anniversary, the Queen and Prince Philip. The visit almost didn't happen as the showground had suffered severe flooding a few days previously, but with the hard work of the staff, they made the day unforgettable. The Royal couple both separated to cover as much of the show as possible, and the obvious delight on the Queen's face was plain for all to see. What a wonderful welcome, and everyone took back memories that would be treasured for a very long time.

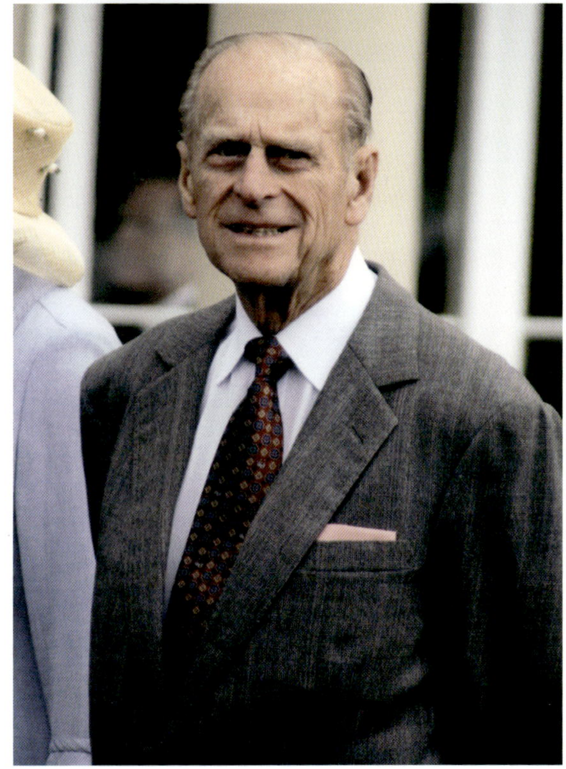

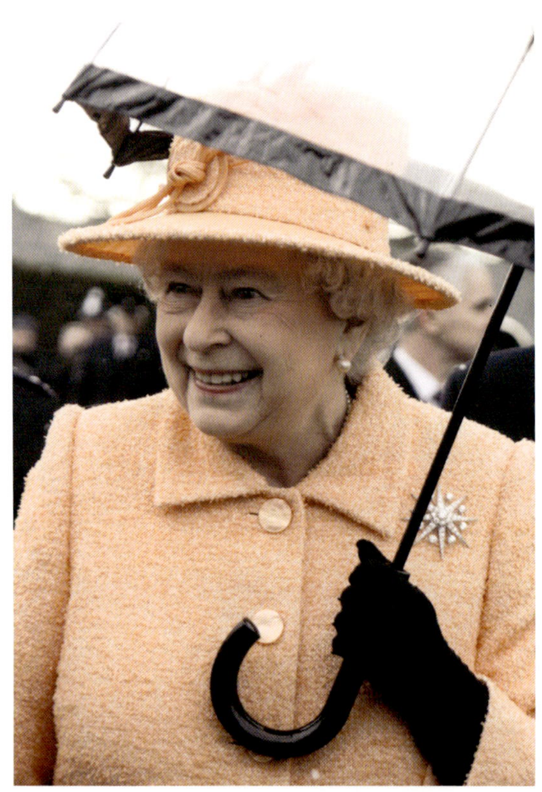

Left:
The Queen, West Newton, February 2009
Her Majesty is pictured here after morning service in the local church. The Sandringham Estate always welcomes the Royal Family, and despite the snowy conditions that day, the Queen looked elegant as she walked past, her trademark umbrella in her gloved hand.

Below:
Prince Charles and the Duchess of Cornwall, February 2009
After visiting the Leeds Grand Theatre, to see the new Assembly Rooms, they undertook a ten-minute walkabout; rather touchingly, the Prince escorted the Duchess to her car as they separated for further visits in the region.

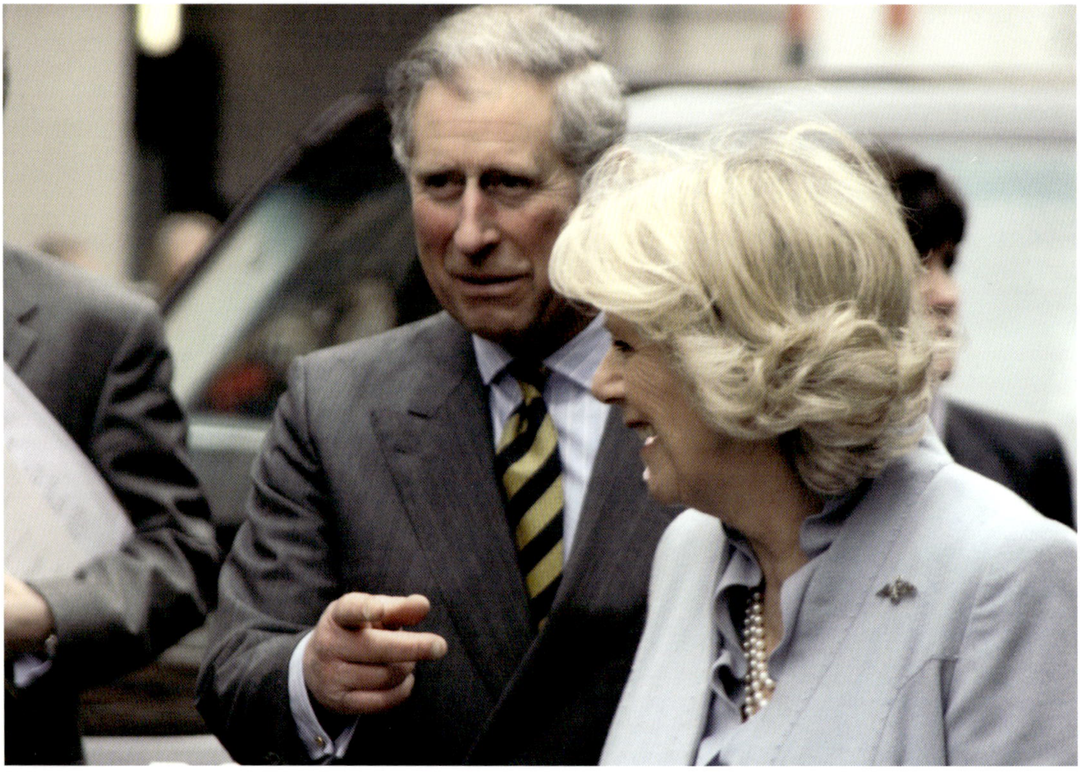